HOW TO SUCCEED AS A FEMALE GUITARIST

The Essential Guide for Working in a Male-Dominated Industry

MW00564914

Vivian Clement

Alfred, the leader in educational publishing,

and the National Guitar Workshop,

one of America's finest guitar schools, have joined

forces to bring you the best, most progressive

educational tools possible. We hope you will enjoy

this book and encourage you to look for

other fine products from Alfred and the

National Guitar Workshop.

Alfred Publishing Co., Inc.
16320 Roscoe Blvd., Suite 100
P.O. Box 10003
Van Nuys, CA 91410-0003
alfred.com

ISBN-10: 0-7390-4304-8 (Book & CD)
ISBN-13: 978-0-7390-4304-2 (Book & CD)

This book was acquired, edited and produced
by Workshop Arts, Inc., the publishing arm of
the National Guitar Workshop.

Nathaniel Gunod, acquisitions, managing editor
Burgess Speed, editor
Matthew Liston, assistant editor
Timothy Phelps, interior design
Ante Gelo, music typesetter
Interior photography by Timothy Phelps; Anthony Paiano; Matthew Liston;
and Stella Jurgen, 17 Designs, Mississauga, Ontario, Canada
Guitars on pages 26 & 27 courtesy of Daisy Rock Guitars
CD recorded by Anthony Paiano at Exodus Studio, Mississauga, Ontario, Canada
Vivian Clement, guitar; Eric Soostar, bass; Paul DeLong, drums; Anthony Paiano, keyboard

Cover photographs: Concert audience © Photographer: Darko Novakovic | Agency: Dreamstime.com
Guitarist © Photographer: Ed Lawrence | Agency: Dreamstime.com
Rock Candy Atomic Pink guitar photo courtesy of Daisy Rock® | DaisyRock.com

TABLE OF CONTENTS

A compact disc is available with this book. Using the disc will help make learning more enjoyable and the information more meaningful. Listening to the CD will help you correctly interpret the rhythms and feel of each example. The symbol at the upper left appears next to each example that is performed on the CD. The track number below each symbol corresponds directly to the example you want to hear. Track 1 will help you tune to this CD.

ABOUT THE AUTHOR

Vivian Clement is a versatile guitarist whose styles range from jazz and blues to pop and rock. She studied jazz with Peter Harris at Humber College in Toronto as well as vocals with classical/pop teacher Helen Knight. She is the author of *Fretboard Knowledge for the Contemporary Guitarist* (Alfred/National Guitar Workshop #21955) and *The Complete Studio Guitarist* (Alfred/National Guitar Workshop #22544). Vivian owns and records at Exodus Studio with her husband Anthony Paiano and keeps busy performing in the Southern Ontario region. She has released three CDs and has taught guitar and vocals for the National Guitar Workshop.

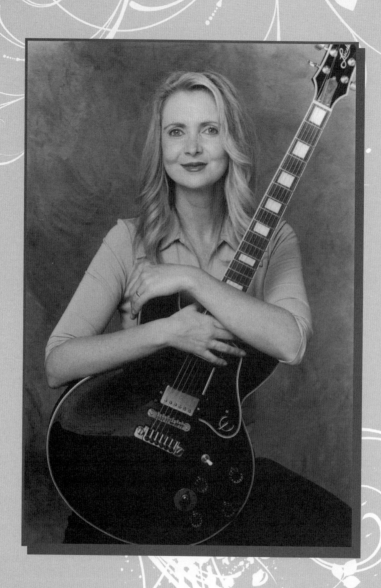

ACKNOWLEDGEMENTS

Thanks to: Burgess Speed, Eric Soostar, Rob Hoinkes, Tish Ciravolo and Daisy Rock Guitars for all of their help, Karissa Read, Timothy Phelps, Janet Billig Rich, Margaret Stowe, Christine Bougie and Regina Zernay.

INTRODUCTION

A recent *Rolling Stone* article listed Joan Jett and Joni Mitchell alongside their male peers as the "100 Greatest Guitarists of All Time." Thanks to the efforts of these pioneers, a new generation of female guitarists is poised to join the pantheon of guitar heroes. From sensitive songwriters like Jewel and Lisa Loeb to aggressive rockers like Allison Robertson and Alexx Calise, more and more women are turning to the guitar for empowerment and self-expression.

This book comes from my experience of over 20 years in the music business as a female guitarist. There are some generalizations made about both men and women that are not meant to offend or promote stereotypes, but to help you prepare for dynamics and situations that you will encounter. I have wanted to write this book for a long time, particularly since I know, firsthand, the importance of having information available for female guitarists who are just starting their musical journeys. When I began my career, no such information existed. I trudged along naively for several years, completely unaware of the hidden dynamics that existed amongst my male colleagues. Much of my female upbringing (as is the case with most women) was working against me. Although I grew up as a tomboy, as an adult I couldn't quite figure out how to work successfully around men. It seemed like there was an unbreakable code of ethics surrounding me that, for all my efforts, I couldn't figure out.

Through much trial and error, I began to discover that men view the workplace and their careers completely different from women. I realized that to succeed in the music business, I needed to learn the rules men adhere to. For instance, men are at home with competition and view it as a game, since they have been competing with each other from a young age. Growing up as a girl, you were undoubtedly given subtle messages that competition amongst friends is inappropriate and can ruin relationships. Men need to be respected for what they do and put their relationships second. Women primarily desire deep relationships and put relationships before their work. Men learn early how to be team players and how to lead when necessary. Women prefer to work with as few people as possible, and generally don't run into many opportunities where they learn effective leadership skills. Even though these slight differences may not seem like a big deal growing up, as adults they can deal a death blow to any woman's musical career.

To succeed as a female guitarist in the music business, you must first and foremost realize that you are entering a *business*. You may sincerely believe that playing guitar is an art form and you should not mix it with business, but the reality is that the minute you start making money you have entered into business. The music business, like all businesses, is structured around the male culture. If you learn the "rules" (which we will discuss throughout this book) and abide by them, you will not only gain the respect needed to catapult your career to the next level, but develop a foundation that will allow for a lifetime of career advancement. You will find that once you have gained the necessary respect from your male peers that you can start integrating some of your female traits without so much resistance. It's important to be open-minded and observe what actually works and what doesn't. For the most part, you will find that most men aren't trying to keep you out of the business, they simply expect everyone to play by the same rules. Throughout this book, I have included tips for working with men in band situations. For more information on working with men, read *Hardball for Women: Winning at the Game of Business* by Pat Heim and Susan K. Golant (Plume).

This book is divided into three parts:

- **Part 1: Knowledge Is Power**, which covers music, gear, performing and recording
- **Part 2: Minding Your Own Business**, which focuses on music as a business
- **Part 3: Successful Female Attitudes**, which covers common mistakes women make, leadership skills, finding your own niche and more

All of these topics play an important role in the female guitarist's development.

This is not a method book, but it will be helpful if you have an understanding of the basics of guitar, such as open chords, major scales, minor scales, standard music notation, TAB and theory. However, if you are not familiar with these, you will still get a lot out of this book. To pursue the basics on your own, check out *Guitar for the Absolute Beginner* by Susan Mazer (#14976) and *The Total Rock Guitarist* by Tobias Hurwitz (#24423), both by Alfred/National Guitar Workshop. All the best and happy guitar playing!

Vivian Clement

Part 1:
Knowledge Is Power

CHAPTER 1
MUSICAL KNOWLEDGE

In Part 1 of this book, we will focus on the importance of musical knowledge. In the past several years, there has been a multitude of young, talented and well-educated guitarists entering the music scene, creating a whole new level of competition. Since the "bar" has been raised, it is important that you equip yourself with as much musical information as you can. One of your goals as a female guitarist should be to become as well-educated as possible in many different topics. Unfortunately, the old adage that women must work twice as hard to achieve half of what a man achieves still applies today.

If you find that you are familiar with some of the following topics, you can use this as an opportunity for review. For unfamiliar topics, you can zero in on any missing gaps in your education. The key is to be sure that you are fairly comfortable with all the fundamentals of music. Everything is built on fundamentals, and gaps in your musical education can be traced back to a deficiency in the basics. For instance, if you don't spend enough time on ear training, specifically on hearing individual intervals, you may find that locating notes on the fretboard can be tricky. The reason for this is that intervals are the foundation upon which everything in music is based.

Photo courtesy of Daisy Rock Guitars

*In 1994, **Lisa Loeb** was the first unsigned artist to top American charts with her single "Stay (I Missed You)," later released on the album* Tails *(1995). She studied piano as a child but later switched to the guitar. (See her interview with the author starting on page 88.)*

The following fundamentals of music will be covered in this chapter.

1. Music notation and theory
2. Chords
3. Right- and left-hand techniques
4. Scales and modes
5. Ear training
6. Improvising (soloing)
7. Singing while you play

This may seem like a lot to learn but if you break things down into smaller chunks and practice them on a daily basis, they will be much easier to master. Concentrate on the areas with which you are most unfamiliar, and as soon as you can, try to integrate them into your playing.

You should work on knowing as many chords as possible. When you learn a new chord, try incorporating it into a song that you already know, or compose a song of your own. You will always memorize things better if you put them in the context of a song. Next, you should spend time on scales, starting with major and minor pentatonics. These two types of scales are very common and can be used in most musical genres. Record a chord progression and try playing the scales over it, or get play-along CDs such as Alfred's *Stand Alone Tracks* series or Glenn Riley's *Jam Guitar: Rock* (Alfred/National Guitar Workshop #23230). Ear training will help you in every aspect of music, so be sure to incorporate it in your daily practice, particularly the area of *lifting* music (learning a song note-for-note), which is the fastest way to develop your ear. Being able to read music is a real plus if you want to become a professional guitarist, so dedicate a few minutes a day to developing this important skill. Finally, improvisation is a big topic where you will need to spend lots of time and study.

Remember, the following theory sections are meant to be a quick reference guide, not an in-depth study. For more information on theory, see *Theory for the Contemporary Guitarist* by Guy Capuzzo (Alfred/National Guitar Workshop #16755).

Band Tip No. 1—Playing the Game

Men and women perceive work from two completely different perspectives. From a man's point of view, work is treated more like a game. All games have rules, strategy and competition. Reaching the goal, whatever that may be, is the primary objective. This also applies in the arena of music, where competence (or being great on your instrument) is how you advance in the ranks.

MUSIC NOTATION

The Staff

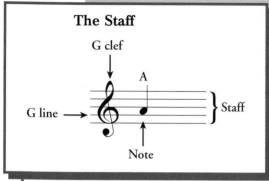

Parts of a Note

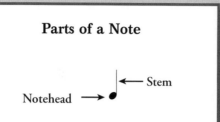

Notes

Note Values

Measures, Bar Lines and Time Signatures

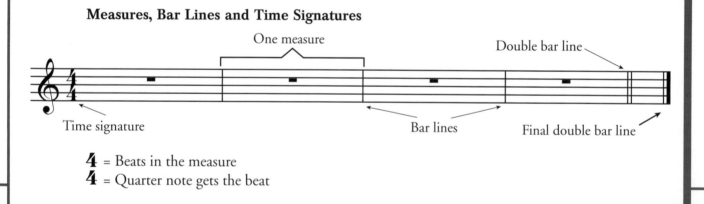

4 = Beats in the measure
4 = Quarter note gets the beat

Ties

When notes are tied, the second note is not struck. Rather, its value is added to that of the first note. So, a half note tied to a quarter note would equal three beats.

Dots

A dot increases the length of a note by one half of its original value. For instance, a half note equals two beats. Half of its value is one beat (a quarter note). So, a dotted half note equals three beats $(2 + 1 = 3)$. A dotted half note is equal to a half note tied to a quarter note. The same logic applies for dotted quarter notes and dotted whole notes.

Rhythmic Notation

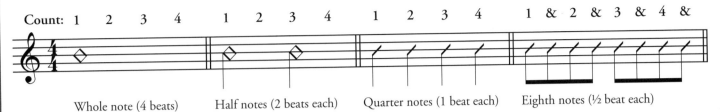

Count: 1 2 3 4   1 2 3 4   1 2 3 4   1 & 2 & 3 & 4 &

Whole note (4 beats)   Half notes (2 beats each)   Quarter notes (1 beat each)   Eighth notes (½ beat each)

Tablature

Tablature (TAB) is a graphic way of writing guitar music. The six lines correspond to the six strings of the guitar (1st line = 1st string, 2nd line = 2nd string, etc.). The numbers on these lines indicate what frets to play. The numbers below the TAB staff tell you which left-hand fingers to use. (Left-hand fingers are numbered 1–4 starting with the index finger.) In this book, the TAB is below the standard music notation.

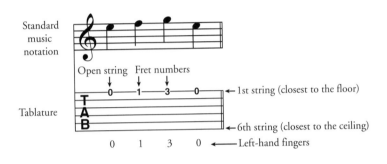

Standard music notation

Open string   Fret numbers

0   1   3   0 ← 1st string (closest to the floor)

Tablature

← 6th string (closest to the ceiling)

0   1   3   0 ← Left-hand fingers

Chord Diagrams

Chord diagrams indicate the fretboard position, shape and fingering of a chord. The hollow dot (O) indicates the root note, the note on which the chord is built and from which it gets its name.

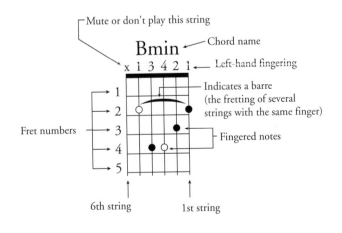

Mute or don't play this string

Bmin ← Chord name

x 1 3 4 2 1 ← Left-hand fingering

Indicates a barre (the fretting of several strings with the same finger)

Fingered notes

Fret numbers → 1 2 3 4 5

6th string   1st string

Scale Diagrams

Scale diagrams are similar to chord diagrams except that they are horizontal rather than vertical.

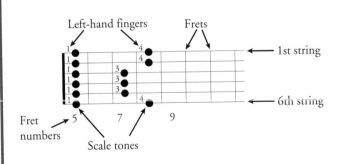

Left-hand fingers   Frets

← 1st string

← 6th string

Fret numbers   5   7   9

Scale tones

MEMORIZING THE FRETBOARD

It can be challenging to learn chords and scales on the entire fretboard if you don't already know the notes. The best way to do this is by using the following system.

Below is a diagram of all the notes of the guitar.

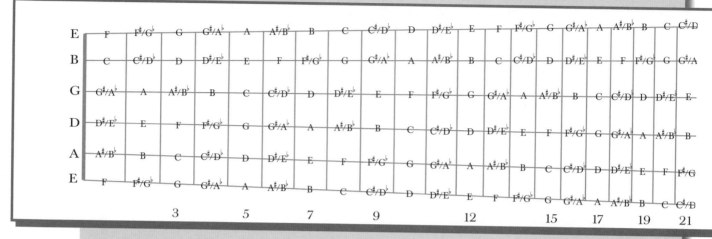

The following diagram illustrates where all of the F notes appear on your fretboard. (This diagram has 24 frets to demonstrate a complete pattern. Not all guitars have 24 frets, so just play as high as you can.) The line that is drawn from note to note reveals the pattern you will be memorizing. The pattern repeats from the 12th to the 24th fret, an octave higher. (It looks like a warped W.)

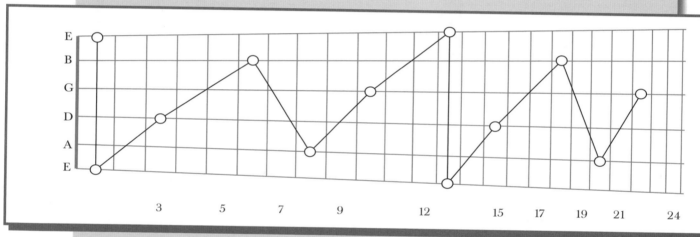

Let's create a numerical sequence and assign each note a number representing its position in relation to all the other F notes. We see that there are six notes in the warped W pattern. By randomly choosing an F note on this graph, you'll be able to find the next F above or below by simply observing which number it is in the sequence and moving up or down in order through the warped W pattern. For example, if you choose the F on the 4th string, 3rd fret—#2 on the sequence—you can find the next F by going down to #1 or up to #3. You can find any note on the fretboard using this pattern.

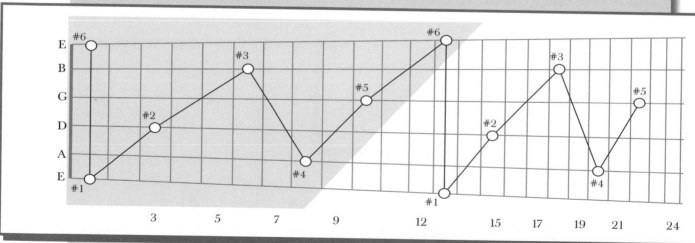

CHORDS

If you have been playing guitar for any amount of time, there is a good chance that you know many of the following chords. Make sure all the notes ring out clearly when you strum them. If you are having difficulty with some of these chords, you may need to develop more strength in your left hand. Go to the next page for strength exercises.

COMMON CHORDS

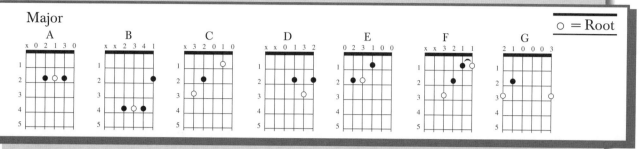

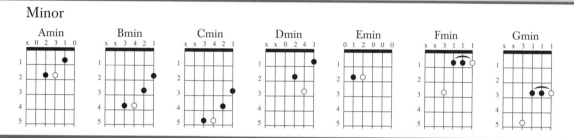

POWER CHORDS

Power chords consist of the root and the 5th of the chord and are used for rock, alternative and punk. These chords are usually played forcefully, with a strong right hand. To get a beefy sound out of these chords, you will need to use a thick pick. Avoid a thin pick, which tends to be too pliable. Learn to play power chords up and down your fretboard, naming the chords at the same time. This will help you memorize them more quickly. (Your index finger will always fall on the root of the chord. That's why it's important to know all the names of the notes of your guitar.)

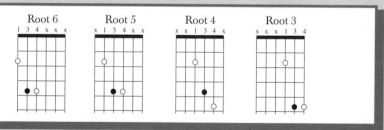

7TH CHORDS AND BEYOND

There are many 7th, 9th, 11th and 13th chords available for the guitarist. Below are some of the most popular. Some of these are more commonly used in jazz, but you'll also come across them in some rock, blues and pop tunes.

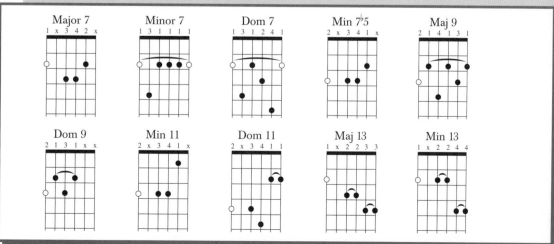

LEFT- AND RIGHT-HAND STRENGTH EXERCISES

Since women generally have smaller hands, the following left-hand exercises will help develop strength and flexibility so you can reach difficult chords with ease. You can use these exercises as warm-ups; this way your hand will be stretched, making the chords easier to execute when you practice. The most difficult chords to play will be the extensions. However, you will find that after you get familiar with them, they will be as easy to play as every other chord you've mastered in the past.

For best results, vary these exercises by using different string groups as well as skipping strings.

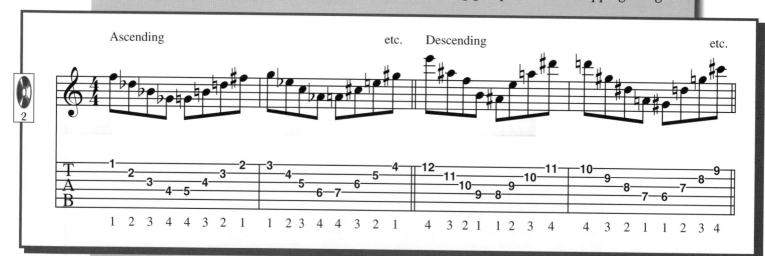

Play the 7th and extension chords below and practice playing them one after the other. Mix them up in any way possible; this will help develop the ability to move your hands wherever they need to go. Practice slowly so chords don't sound sloppy. Try different rhythms with your right hand. All notes on each string should be clear and not muffled.

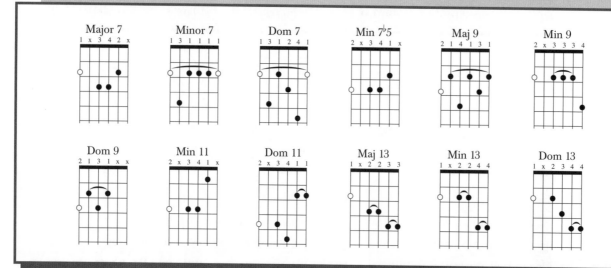

Band Tip No. 2—Competency

Initially, a woman needs to be competent at her instrument to be welcomed into the male culture. Competency may open the door to opportunity, but it is only the beginning of being successful. There are many other elements that need to be present for advancement such as being a team player, talking shop, self-promotion and being assertive.

THE ART OF SOLOING

Bonnie Raitt, renowned for her slide blues guitar playing, did not reach commercial success until the release of her 10th album, *Nick of Time.* The moral of the story is to stick with it and not get discouraged if recognition is slow to come.

Men, for the most part, have dominated the field of guitar improvisation (also referred to as *soloing*). Only recently have women stepped up to the plate to take their place as contenders, but they have not received much media attention. Fortunately, this is beginning to change. Being a great lead player is the one area that will make you stand out from other guitar players, particularly because you are a woman. At the present time, being a female guitarist is still a novelty, and this skill alone can be used to open great doors of opportunity. Therefore, learning to improvise is an area in which you'll need to spend much of your practice time. Although it takes many years to become a great improviser, it is well worth the effort. There is nothing more rewarding as a guitarist than to feel that you have command of your instrument, particularly in the area of improvisation.

It's important to listen to a lot of guitar solos in various styles. Listen to the older guitar players, not just the new ones. And be open to different styles, not just your favorite. The best way to start is to listen to fairly easy solos. Then, learn how to play them, increasing the difficulty with each new solo. Any time you learn a solo, you should always make an effort to transcribe it (see page 14).

As far as developing your own solos, just remember that improvising is a lot like storytelling. You don't just want to ramble on with a whole bunch of notes; you want to aim at playing something meaningful. One important dynamic to consider is your *phrasing.* Phrasing refers to the manner in which you execute your notes. As when speaking, variety is important. For instance, there are times when you want to play slowly and times you want to play quickly. You may want to play a lot of notes, or just keep it simple. The key is to keep the listener in mind. You don't want to sound too monotonous or perform the same thing over and over. Eventually, you'll develop your own unique and recognizable style of phrasing.

Suggested Listening:

Blues	Rock	Jazz	Acoustic
B. B. King	Yngwie Malmsteen	George Benson	Ani DiFranco
Jonny Lang	Amy Schugar	Mimi Fox	Kaki King
Bonnie Raitt	Steve Vai	Joe Pass	Preston Reed
Stevie Ray Vaughan	Eddie Van Halen	Emily Remler	Adrian Legg

LIFTING AND TRANSCRIBING TUNES

Lifting a song is the ability to hear music and then perform it on your instrument. This is a great way to assimilate other guitarists' solos. You can then pick out certain riffs that you really like and add them to your own repertoire.

The best way to lift a solo is by being very familiar with it. Play a recording of the solo over and over until you can sing it from memory. Start with an easy song that you can learn in one sitting. If you have a "looping" feature on your CD, loop the solo and sing it over and over. You will find that if you can sing a solo from memory, playing it will be a lot easier. For any difficult parts, zero in and loop just that part and sing it. There is also computer software that allows you to record a song and then slow it down for easy learning.

Band Tip No. 3—Make Friends with the Staff

Whenever you work at a bar, make the effort to befriend the staff, particularly the waitresses and bartenders who are serving you. They play a big role in influencing the owner of the establishment on whether or not you should be hired again. Some women can be threatened by a talented and independent woman, so it is in your best interest to make friends with them. Nothing seals a friendship better than a nice tip at the end of the night. If you were given a discount on food and drinks, it's not inconceivable to tip as high as 20 to 25%. The waitress will appreciate it, since that is how she makes her living, and chances are you'll get a good review.

Don't stop at just learning solos. Learn the chords to the whole song. Listen for the chord progressions and try to hear the patterns throughout the song. For example, you may hear that there are I–IV–V progressions at the start of each verse. (For more on chord progressions, see page 22.)

Transcribing music is when you listen to music and write it out note-for-note exactly the way the artist is performing it. If you can't notate music yet, just write it out in TAB for now. Transcribing is a good way to keep track of all the solos that you learn as you go along. You can also file them in a binder for future reference. You can then use your binder when you are jamming with other musician friends or for future performances. Once you become adept at simple songs and solos, aim for songs that are a little more challenging. You'll discover that the more solos you transcribe, the better your ear will become.

Lifting and transcribing other guitarists' solos is by far the quickest way to absorb their playing style and technique. Additionally, you will have to stretch your playing abilities, since some of the riffs you learn will be beyond your present abilities. Although you can buy books of transcribed solos, you should always learn songs on your own by ear. There are too many subtle nuances contained in a solo that cannot be illustrated in a book.

GUITAR TECHNIQUES

Now, let's cover some important guitar techniques. If you are having difficulties with some of these techniques, it simply means you need to build more strength in your left hand. You may also consider checking the *action* on the neck of your guitar (the action is the height of the strings from the neck of the guitar). If the action is too high, some techniques will require more strength. Also check the gauge (thickness) of your strings. If you're a beginner, you should use a fairly light gauge of string. As your left hand gets stronger, increase the gauge. For electric guitar you can start with .009 and move up to .011 gauge. The thicker the string, the better the tone of the guitar. Be sure to check the positioning of your thumb. Make sure it is not too high up on the back of the neck; keep it in the middle. This position will allow your fingers to have greater reach. Also, use a thick pick for better right-hand control.

HAMMER-ON

To play a *hammer-on,* pick the first note then sound the second note on the same string by quickly "hammering" a left-hand finger onto the appropriate fret. (You are only using your right hand to produce the first note; the second note is produced by the hammer-on itself.)

Following is an exercise that will help you execute hammer-ons successfully.

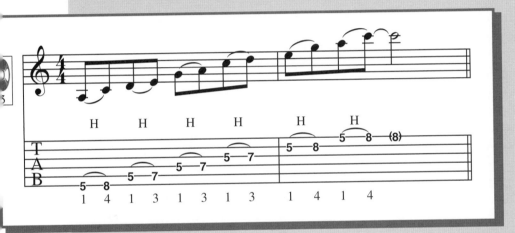

$\underset{\smile}{H}$ = Hammer-on

PULL-OFFS

These are like hammer-ons in reverse. Your left hand holds down two notes simultaneously on the same string; for example, your 4th finger on the 8th fret and your 1st finger on the 5th fret. After you strike the string with your pick, sound the second note by quickly pulling your other left-hand finger away. Try the following exercise to build your left hand for pull-offs.

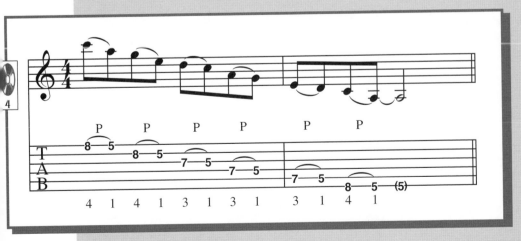

$\underset{\smile}{P}$ = Pull-off

With both hammer-ons and pull-offs, make sure all the notes are equal in volume. This will take practice.

BENDS

A *bend* is the "pushing up" or "pulling down" of a string to affect its pitch. When bending, it is good to use additional fingers for reinforcement. If you are bending the 1st string, you should bend (or push) it *upward*. When you're bending the 6th string, bend (or pull) it *downward*. The other strings can go in either direction, depending on what you're playing. Be sure not to over- or under-extend the bend. Stop at the correct pitch—a quarter step, half step, whole step or a whole step plus a half step.

♩ = Bend

VIBRATO

This is a common technique used by blues and rock players and is really a series of quick, tiny bends that produce a warbling effect often used by singers. *Vibrato* can be slow or quick depending on the desired effect, but the key is to create evenness in the effect. The rhythm and distance of the bends need to be consistent. You can use two or three fingers to achieve this effect. You can also move your wrist back and forth as you are moving the strings.

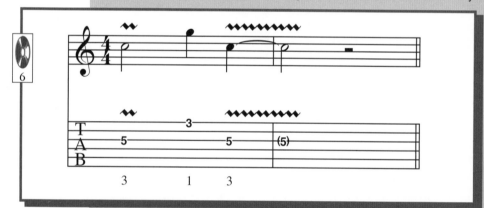

∿∿∿ = Vibrato

SLIDES

Slides are one of the simplest guitar techniques around and are very effective in adding character to a solo. Simply place one of your left-hand fingers on the string and pick it with your right hand. While the note is still ringing, move the left-hand finger up or down the neck. You can slide as little or as far as you want, as long as the note you finally land on fits with the chord that is being played. (Your ear will be able to tell if the note is right or not). You also want to keep the beat of the song in mind, so it sounds in time.

SL
⟋ = Ascending slide

SL
⟍ = Descending slide

SCALES

Scales are the fundamental building blocks of improvising. The *major scale* is the most important scale, from which all other scales are derived. Each note in the major scale is referred to using a *scale degree* number: 1 (or Root)–2–3–4–5–6–7. Major scales always have the same pattern of whole steps (W) and half steps (H): W–W–H–W–W–W–H. You can construct a major scale starting on any note by following this pattern. Below is an example of a C Major scale.

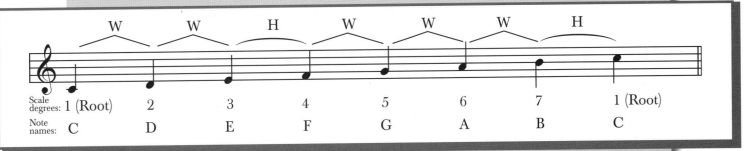

MAJOR PENTATONIC

A *pentatonic* scale is a five-note scale. The *major pentatonic* scale is commonly used in pop, rock, country and blues and can be played in any key by moving the root to the desired notes. The major pentatonic scale contains the scale degrees 1–2–3–5–6. Following are five major pentatonic scale patterns.

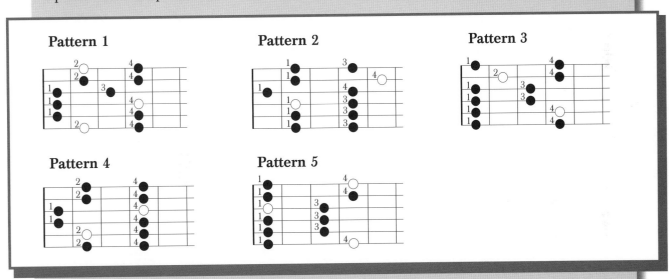

Below is an example of a solo using a major pentatonic scale. Use Track 9 so you can try your own soloing with this great scale. In this example, you will see *grace notes*. Grace notes appear as tiny notes (♪) before a regular-sized note. They should be played as an ornament to the note that follows, with no rhythmic value of their own. Measure 4 uses *double stops*. A double stop is two notes played at the same time. They can be played using *hybrid picking*, where you play the 3rd string with your pick and the 1st string with the 2nd finger of your right hand.

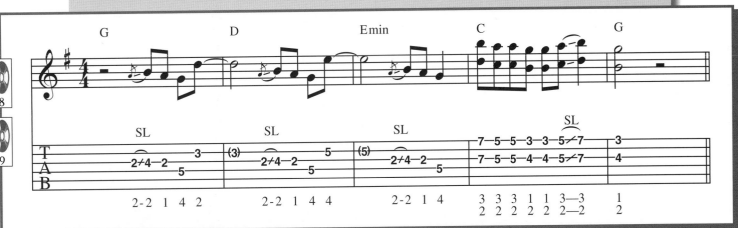

MINOR PENTATONIC

The *minor pentatonic* scale has a more "bluesy" sound to it. It is used extensively in pop, rock, country, blues, alternative music and punk. It is perhaps the most widely used scale because it fits so many musical situations and almost always sounds "right." It uses the scale degrees 1–♭3–4–5–♭7.

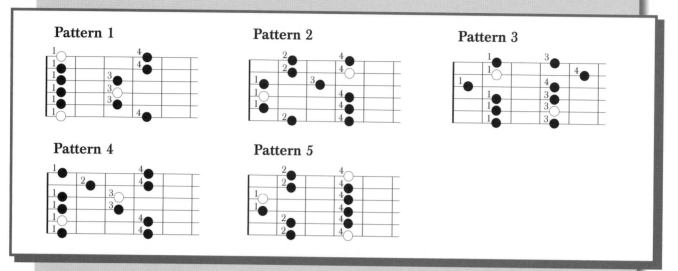

The example below is a solo using the minor pentatonic scale. Take time to practice your own pentatonic solo using Track 11 as accompaniment.

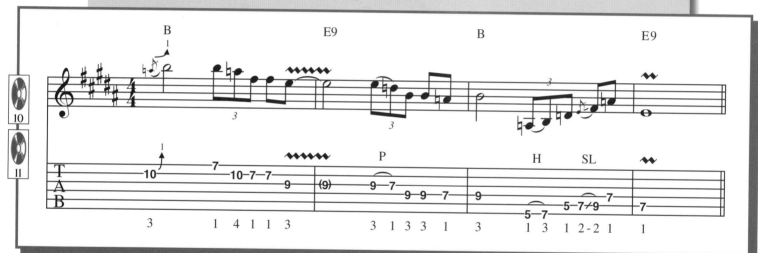

Band Tip No. 4—Understanding Men

You don't need to act like a man in order to be accepted as part of the band. The most important thing to understand is the exclusive dynamics that exist amongst your male musicians. One of the best ways to do this is to observe how men interact with each other. Also, finding a mentor (a male friend who will help) is also very beneficial.

MODES

There are seven *modes* of the major scale, each one starting on a different scale degree. The modes all have their own distinctive sound and can be used over various chord progressions. A common fingering for each mode is shown below, with the scale degrees listed above each diagram. These scale degrees reflect a *parallel* approach to the modes; this means you designate the first note of the mode as 1, the 2nd as 2, etc.

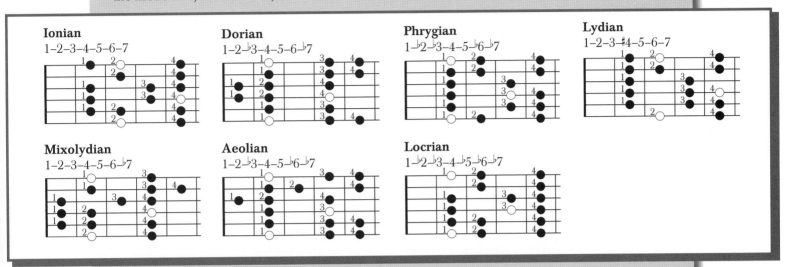

Following are examples of how you can use modes over different chord progressions. As you become familiar with modes, you'll instinctively know which ones to use over which progressions. Each example is followed by an accompanying track where you can experiment on your own. The Dorian example uses *swing eighths*, which are written like regular eighth notes but sound like a triplet with the first two eighth notes tied together (♫ = ♫³). In this book, the swing eighths rhythm is indicated with the symbol: *Swing 8ths.*

Dorian

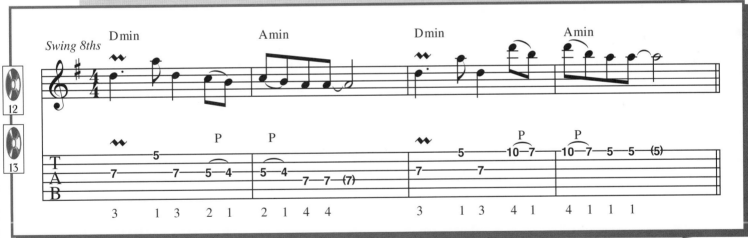

Aeolian

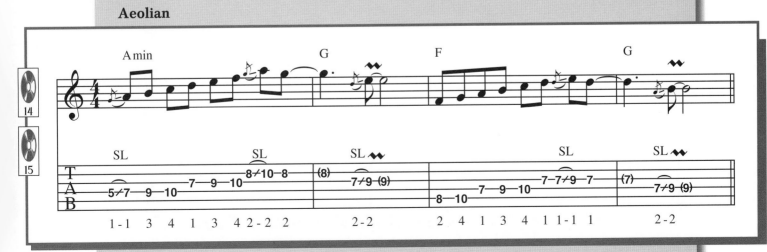

EAR TRAINING

Ear training helps you recognize intervals, scales, chords and chord progressions upon hearing them. The importance of ear training cannot be overemphasized. It is no coincidence that great musicians also have great ears.

It is important to integrate ear training into your daily practice routine. You can do this not only when practicing with your instrument, but any time you hear music on the radio or in a public place. By becoming an active music listener, rather than a passive one, you'll notice that your ability to recognize chords and progressions will greatly increase. The results of this effort will undoubtedly begin surfacing in your practice and performances.

PRACTICING INTERVALS

Whenever you are practicing intervals, be sure to sing them while playing them on your guitar. Find the locations for all the intervals across the entire fretboard, including octaves, above or below the given examples. As you play each interval, sing the actual name of the interval at the same time. This way you are simultaneously learning the interval names and training your ear to recognize the sounds of the intervals. The following exercises will help you get started in your ear training, but for a more in-depth study, refer to *Ear Training for the Contemporary Guitarist* by Jody Fisher (Alfred/National Guitar Workshop #19370).

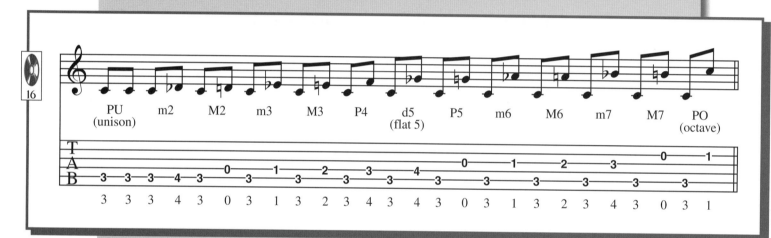

Abbreviation	Interval	Distance in Half Steps
PU	perfect unison	0
m2	minor 2nd	1
M2	major 2nd	2
m3	minor 3rd	3
M3	major 3rd	4
P4	perfect 4th	5
d5	diminished 5th	6
P5	perfect 5th	7
m6	minor 6th	8
M6	major 6th	9
m7	minor 7th	10
M7	major 7th	11
PO	perfect octave	12

Band Tip No. 5—Speak Up!

Don't be afraid to voice your opinion on band issues (or any issues) if you don't agree on something. You don't need to be a diva and get over-emotional, but you do need to take your stand on issues and speak with confidence. Of course, you need to have the discretion to know when you should simply follow the decisions of your bandleader.

SCALES AND CHORDS

Take a scale or mode from pages 17–19 and play it on your guitar while simultaneously singing the names of the notes. You can alter your voice to a higher or lower octave where necessary. Singing and playing together is an effective way of internalizing scales. It makes it easier and quicker to memorize them since you are using different parts of your memory to accomplish this. You can use this same technique when you practice chords. Practice all your chords naming and singing the notes individually. This will also help you recognize different chord *inversions* (fingerings of a chord with a note other than the root as the lowest note).

Below is an example of how you can practice ear training using scales and chords.

DIATONIC HARMONY

To understand the next section (Hearing Chord Progressions, page 22), we need to take a quick look at *diatonic harmony*. This is the study of chords based on the major scale. Each chord is assigned an upper- or lower-case Roman numeral based on which scale degree is its root. For example, in the key of C Major, a C Major chord (built on scale degree 1) is indicated by Roman numeral I, a D Minor chord (scale degree 2), Roman numeral ii, and so forth (see below). A lower-case Roman numeral indicates a minor chord, while upper-case is used for major chords. The vii° chord is a special case; the small circle means it is a *diminished* chord. All major scales have the same pattern of major, minor and diminished chords.

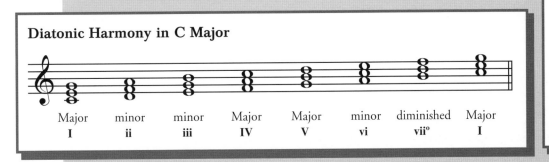

Roman Numerals	
I or i	1
II or ii	2
III or iii	3
IV or iv	4
V or v	5
VI or vi	6
VII or vii	7

HEARING CHORD PROGRESSIONS

Learning to recognize different chord progressions by ear takes practice but is a very valuable tool. Since most chord progressions are simple patterns, you'll soon become familiar with them. One method that works well is to listen to the bass player in a song, because the bass player usually plays the roots of the chords. You can then zero in on the quality of the chords. For example, learn to differentiate if a chord is major (sounds happy), minor (sounds melancholy) or dominant (sounds bright). The following are examples of common chord progressions found in different genres of music.

I–IV–V

You'll find this chord progression in most contemporary genres like pop, blues, reggae and R&B. Here is an example of a reggae tune using a I–IV–V progression. Use an A Major Pentatonic or A Major scale to solo over Track 19.

I–vi–IV–V

This progression is also found in contemporary music. Sometimes there is a variation where a I–vi–ii–V is played (the ii replaces the IV and is a minor chord). This next example features an acoustic guitar on the CD. Jam over Track 21 using the G Major Pentatonic or G Major scale.

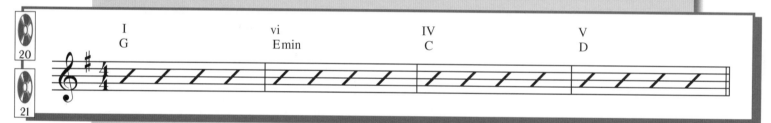

ii–V–I

The ii–V–I progression makes up the bulk of jazz music. The ii is minor, the V is dominant and the I is usually a major 7th or a minor 7th chord. Listen to this progression and you'll be able to immediately identify it as being in the jazz genre. Solo over Track 23 using the scales indicated below the staff.

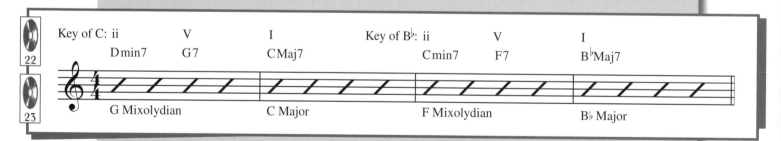

READING CHARTS

Being able to read music is very important if you want to have opportunities as a professional guitarist. Like everything else in music education, reading takes time. The best way to practice reading charts is to buy a few books and spend time in your daily practice working on them. The following *chart* (song notated with everything you need for performance) is a *12-bar blues* (a very common chord progression that is 12 measures long and uses primarily the I, IV and V chords) in the style of Tracy Chapman's "Give Me One Reason." Let's take a look at how to read this chart.

1. After the title, you'll see an indication of the style of the song. This song is a Medium Rock Blues.

2. The *tempo* (how fast the song is to be played) is indicated directly below the style. In this case, the tempo is 110 quarter notes per minute.

3. This song is in the key of G as is indicated by the F♯ in the key signature. You'll probably notice that F♮ is used instead of F♯ throughout the song; this is normal for the blues and does not change the fact that the song is in G.

4. Next to the key signature is the time signature, which is $\frac{4}{4}$.

5. The song starts with an intro guitar fill for two bars followed by a repeat sign at the 3rd bar. At the end of 12 bars, there is another repeat sign indicating that you are to repeat the song starting from the first repeat sign (bar 3).

6. The *chords symbols* (G7, C7, D7, etc.) above the staff indicate the chords to use when playing rhythm guitar. The notes on the staff form the actual melody of the song.

Give Me Those Raisins

EFFECTIVE PRACTICING HABITS

No matter what you study on the guitar, unless you have a regular practice routine (reviewing old and learning new material), your progress will be slow. Consistent practice is vital for the advancing guitarist. Even if you are naturally gifted, chances are that someone with lesser abilities will surpass you if they have better practicing habits.

Arrange your practice time around your work or school schedule. The best way to do this is to plan out your practicing time at the start of your week. By pre-planning, you can better gauge your progress so you won't get stuck in a rut. Determine ahead of time what topics you will be focusing on rather than just noodling and wasting valuable time. Buy a planner and write out the days and hours that you will dedicate to practicing. For instance, on Monday you may have three hours free, but on Tuesday you may only have one hour. Thursday and Friday you might be busy, but Saturday you have all afternoon. The key is to keep the momentum going and to be as realistic with your time as possible. Even if you don't follow your plan exactly, you will accomplish a lot more than if you hadn't planned at all. It's also a good idea to take one or two days off a week so you won't feel overworked. Resting allows you to feel fresh when you get back on your instrument.

There are many ways to practice your guitar. Find a routine that works for you and alter it to suit your needs. Below is a sample practice routine.

1. Make a habit of always assuring that your guitar is tuned properly, by using either a tuning fork or a tuner.
2. Spend five minutes reviewing the notes of your guitar up and down the fretboard. (Use the system on page 10.)
3. Spend the next 10 minutes or so reviewing what you practiced the day before. It's tempting to skip this part, but this discipline alone will greatly speed up your progress.
4. Practice your left- and right-hand techniques using a metronome.
5. Focus on a few scales that you want to learn and be sure to play them slowly. Use your metronome and increase the speed incrementally each day. Always practice with correct technique. At some point, you will find that by increasing the speed you will hit a wall where your playing becomes sloppy. Decrease the tempo until you are playing accurately again. Repeat this process as you increase the speed, never playing above your ability. Remember that practice doesn't make perfect—*perfect practice* makes perfect!
6. Review chords you may be having some difficulty with. Work on left-hand stretches.
7. Always add new chords to your repertoire. Practice changing from chord to chord until you can execute them cleanly.
8. Lift or transcribe some new music, or review some of your past transcriptions.
9. Add songs from different genres to your repertoire whenever possible. This is called *repertoire development.*

On days you don't have a lot of time, you can split this routine into two parts. But always be sure to have your guitar tuned and review your previous practice before each session.

SINGING AND PLAYING

You may not desire to be a vocalist, but it is quite advantageous to your career if you can do some singing; any musician who also sings has more opportunities for gigs. This added ability, though, does present some challenges. It can be tricky to sing and play lead guitar, particularly if you have foot pedals. Jumping into a solo right after singing the last note of the chorus—without missing a beat—takes a little bit of practice and experience.

Here are some tips for singing while playing guitar and using foot pedals:

1. Use a boom stand instead of a straight mic stand to give yourself room to maneuver your guitar.

2. Position your amplifier behind you, aimed towards your ears, either by using an amp stand or the adjustable "arms" on the side of the amp that allow you to tilt it upwards. (If you don't have these arms, they can be purchased at a music store.) Put a monitor in front of you that is also tilted toward your ears. This is so you can hear your guitar and voice together above the rest of the band. This will allow you to focus on your performance rather than trying to find the sound of your vocals or guitar.

3. If you are using foot pedals, place them between yourself and your boom stand, close to your feet so you have easy access to turn them on or off. You also want to be able to take a quick glance down at them so you can move your foot around. If you are using analog pedals, it is easy for you to see which pedals you're stomping on. If instead you are using digital pedals, which have different banks for the effects, keep the most common banks in the front of the chain, therefore you don't have to search for them before a solo. (See page 30 to learn more about effects.)

4. Although high heels can be really stylish, they quickly become uncomfortable with a ten-pound guitar on your shoulder. Also, high heels can be tricky when trying to feel around for your pedals. Therefore, choose footwear that's comfortable and won't kill your feet at the end of the night. If you want to use really nice shoes, bring a few extra pairs with varying heel heights to give your feet a break.

5. Also consider purchasing a wide leather guitar strap. The wider the strap, the better weight distribution on your shoulders and back.

6. Be sure to do vocal warm-ups as well as guitar warm-ups before playing. You can do this by simultaneously practicing scales and vocalizing them. This is a time-saver that can be really helpful before a show.

Vocal Warm-Ups

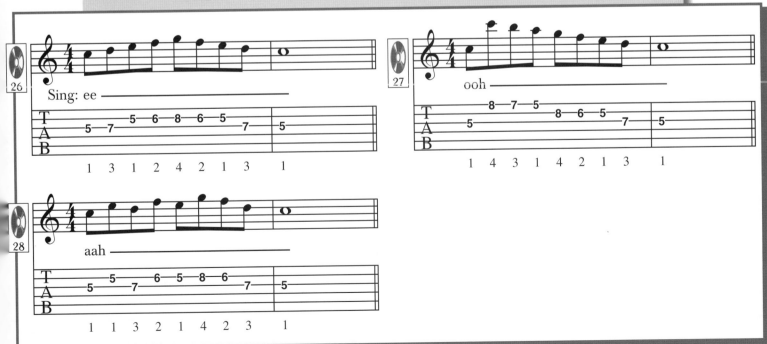

CHAPTER 2
TECHNICAL KNOWLEDGE

Throughout your career, you will probably own a lot of different types of equipment. Although you may start out with just the basic guitar and amp, as time progresses and your opportunities expand, you will need more gear. In this chapter, we will cover the technical knowledge you will need as a guitarist.

ELECTRIC GUITARS

Let's take a look at the different types of guitars that are on the market today. The two obvious categories are electric and acoustic, but there is a lot of variety in each type. Although certain guitars are used for specific genres of music, that doesn't always have to be the case. The most important consideration is finding a guitar that is comfortable for you (not too heavy or big) and is in good working condition.

As far as electric guitars go, there are two categories: *solid body* and *hollow body*. The solid body is by far the most popular choice for contemporary music. In this category, there are guitars with *single-coil pickups, double-coil pickups* (also known as *humbuckers*) or combinations of both. Guitarists often choose single-coil pickups if they're playing funk and blues because of their bright, clean tone. An example of a single-coil guitar would be a Fender Stratocaster. Double-coil guitars are used by guitarists who want a beefier, heavier rock sound. An example of a double-coil guitar is a Gibson Les Paul. Many jazz guitarists prefer using hollow body guitars. (Within the category of hollow bodies, there are also semi-hollow body guitars.) The reason jazz guitarists prefer hollow bodies is because the sound is more mellow and warm, which is very appropriate for this genre of music.

Single-coil guitar.

Double-coil guitar.

Semi-hollow body guitar.

ACOUSTIC GUITARS

Many players start out playing an acoustic guitar. This helps build left-hand strength because the action on the neck is higher than on an electric guitar. Even if you didn't start playing on an acoustic guitar, at some point you'll probably want to own one. Most acoustics have six strings, but there are also 12-string guitars. (There are 12-string electrics as well, but the acoustics are more common.) *Classical guitars* (also called *nylon-string guitars*) have a sweet, mellow tone. Both acoustic and classical guitars can be purchased with pickups, which are very useful for live performance and recording.

When looking to purchase an acoustic guitar, try to get one with a solid wood top, as opposed to a laminate or plywood top. Having a solid top will give your guitar a much nicer tone. You may also decide to get a *cutaway* which allows your fingers easy access past the 12th fret. Since you will often play the acoustic guitar while sitting, make sure the guitar isn't too big and that it balances evenly on your lap. If your guitar is too big or heavy, you will also find it difficult to play while standing for performances. Recently, companies have been designing lighter and slimmer guitars with women in mind.

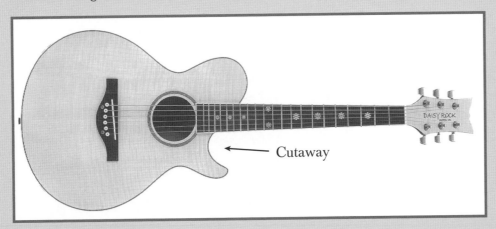
Cutaway

Acoustic guitar with cutaway.

Band Tip No. 8—Take Care of Your Gear

Part of being professional on your instrument is having a general knowledge of how to maintain your gear; if something goes wrong at a gig, you may be able to fix the problem yourself. Ask a friend who is familiar with guitar and amp repairs to teach you some basics, and practice doing some of the repairs yourself at home. You can leave the real tricky stuff to a repair guy, but fundamental knowledge will be very helpful.

AMPLIFIERS

Even though there are a lot of amplifiers on the market today, they all fall into one of the following three categories: tube, solid state or hybrid. *Tube amplifiers* have been around the longest and get their name because that they use vacuum tubes in their design. They have a much warmer sound than solid state or hybrid. Tube amplifiers are considered more vintage-sounding and are often preferred by blues, rock and country players. *Solid-state amplifiers* use transistors instead of tubes and usually cost a little less. They are a lot lighter than tube amplifiers. Jazz players often prefer solid-state amplifiers for their clean sound and ample *headroom* (meaning they don't distort until turned up very loud). *Hybrid amplifiers* use a combination of solid-state and tube technology, usually a tube preamp (to add vintage-sounding warmth to the sound) and solid-state power amplifier (which makes the signal from the preamp louder). *Modeling amplifiers* are a form of hybrid in that they combine analog with digital technology. Modeling amplifiers have a DSP (digital signal processing) feature that can emulate many of the traditional amplifier sounds. Hybrid amps are very versatile and provide a lot of bang for your buck.

Modeling amps combine analog with digital technology to emulate many vintage and modern tones.

Since tubes are made from glass, they need to be treated with special care. If your tubes seem frosty or have a bluish hue, you should change them fairly soon.

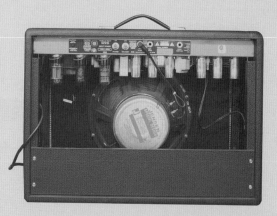

AMP CONFIGURATIONS

As well as the three different categories of amplifiers (tube, solid state and hybrid), there are also three configurations of amplifiers: combo, head plus cabinet and rackmount plus cabinet. *Combo amplifiers* are the most compact of the three and have all of their components inside one cabinet, including one or more speakers. The *head plus cabinet* combination is popular among guitarists who want to mix and match different cabinets and heads for the purpose of achieving different sounds. The *rackmount plus cabinet* is a very flexible combination, since you can change the signal chain of the circuitry, allowing for many options of sounds. This amp is useful in a studio situation where getting different effects may be desirable.

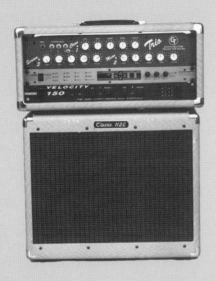 

With the head plus cabinet combination,
you can mix and match your
heads and cabinets.

Some combo amplifiers have great tones
(especially the vintage or reissue amps).
Unfortunately, they are not as versatile
as rackmounts or heads.

Band Tip No. 9—Be Prepared

For your gigs, it's a good idea to bring along a small tool kit for any emergencies. It should include lots of extra strings, extra guitar cables and an adapter (if you use foot pedals). Also bring a small power strip, fuses for your amp and spare tubes (put the tubes in a protective container since they can be easily broken). You should also have a small screwdriver and needle-nose pliers with wire cutters (to use when changing your strings). All of this can fit into a guitar gig bag that has extra zippers on the sides or front.

GUITAR EFFECTS

At some point, after you've purchased a guitar and an amp, you'll want to look into picking up a few *guitar effects*. The type of effects you buy will depend largely on the type of music you are playing.

There are two types of guitar effects: analog and digital. The analog effects are often referred to as *stomp boxes*. They are rather inexpensive and simple to use. Digital effects are usually referred to as *multi-effect units* and contain many effects in one. They can be either foot pedals or rackmount units (which may also come with a foot controller). Analog stomp boxes usually have only one effect per unit. So if you want a lot of effects, you will have to get a lot of separate stomp boxes. Because the digital units feature a variety of effects, they tend to be more popular. Some of the digital units attempt to copy the exact sounds of analog stomp boxes, though many guitarists feel they still tend to sound somewhat digital.

If you plan on getting into recording, digital effects come in quite handy, since they produce less "noise" than stomp boxes. They are a little more complicated to use, and you'll need to do some programming to suit your needs. Of course, you can use digital effects for live performance as well. Sometimes stomp boxes are the easier solution, particularly if you are singing in the band and don't want to have your attention diverted into too many different directions. Because a stomp box has only one effect, you will always know which box to press to get that effect. For digital units, you will need to find the sound that you are looking for by pressing on the unit until the right sound is selected.

Guitar effects fall into three categories: *signal enhancers* (EQ, compression, distortion, wah-wah), time-based effects (chorus, pitch shift, delay, flanger) and ambient effects (reverb and certain types of delay that affect time and ambience).

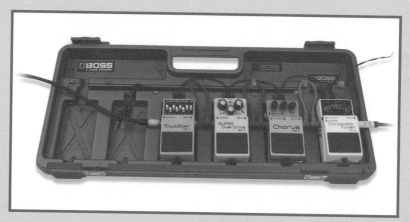

You can purchase fairly inexpensive individual stomp boxes to meet your effects needs.

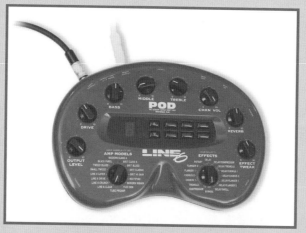

Digital multi-effects units have come a long way in producing a fairly authentic simulation of the original stomp boxes and amp sounds.

Band Tip No. 10—Choose Quality Equipment

When buying equipment, you're better off waiting until you have enough money for good quality brand names. Not only is it a better guarantee that you won't have problems down the road, but it sends the message that you understand quality and the meaning of being professional. If you can't presently afford a good instrument, work with what you have and make it one of your future goals.

THE SIGNAL CHAIN

There is a logical sequence in which effects are placed. You won't have to worry about this when it comes to digital effects, since the chain is organized for you already. As far as stomp boxes go, you'll need to know which order to put them in for the best results (see below).

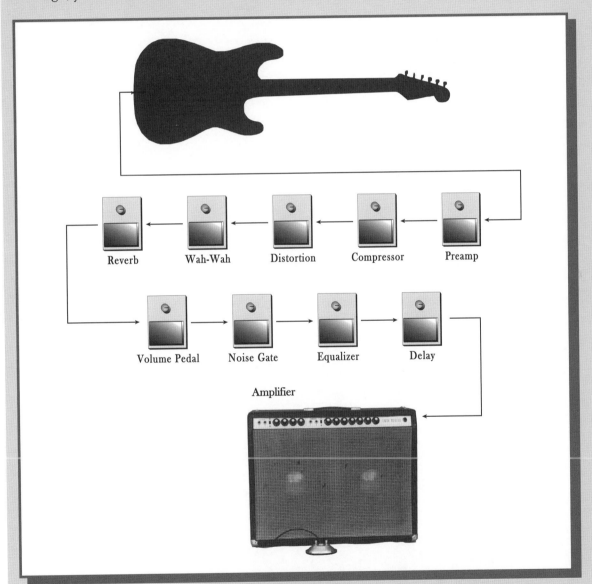

Reverb Wah-Wah Distortion Compressor Preamp

Volume Pedal Noise Gate Equalizer Delay

Amplifier

One thing to keep in mind when purchasing effects is that a little goes a long way. It's tempting, particularly if you've never owned effects before, to go overboard and spend your money buying a whole bunch of new gear. But you will notice that experienced guitarists use these units to enhance their sound rather then draw too much attention to the effects themselves.

OPERATING A SOUND SYSTEM

You may or may not decide to own a *public address system* (PA for short) for amplifying live sound, but at some point in your career you will probably run into a situation where you will need to know how to use one. They are pretty straightforward to operate. A PA consists of:

1. Mics

There are studio mics and performance mics. A performance mic is also referred to as a *dynamic mic.*

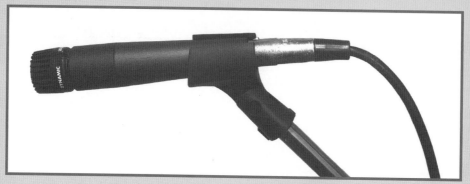

Dynamic microphones are the industry standard and very popular for live performances as well as recording instruments in the studio.

2. Cables for the mics, instruments, speakers and monitors

There are different cables for different applications. A mic cable is also called an XLR cable because of the connector, or jack, at the end of the cable (see Fig. 1 below). The end of the microphone has three pins (also called a male connector) which are inserted into the end of the XLR cable (female connector). The other end of the cable has the opposite (male connector), which are inserted into the mixer (female connector). Instrument cables, also called ¼ inch cables or guitar cords, have two ends that look identical (see Fig. 2). These can be used for guitars, keyboards and bass. Speaker and monitor cables have the same ends as instrument cables. Sometimes, the cable itself is flat and looks like two joined cables running parallel with each other, but sometimes it looks exactly like an instrument cable. Speaker/monitor cables and instrument cables differ internally. If you purchase these different types of cables, be sure to label them. You can use an instrument cable as a speaker cable in a pinch, but only at a low volume. But you shouldn't use a speaker/monitor cable for an instrument because it is not shielded and will generate a lot of noise.

Fig. 1: XLR cable.

Fig. 2: Guitar cable.

3. Mixer or soundboard

A mixer (or mixing board) is the unit into which you plug all your mics and speakers. Mixing boards may look different from one company to the next, but generally, they will have the same components. The typical mixing board is divided into three different sections according to function:

1. **Individual channel strips.** Each instrument or microphone should have its own channel so you can control it separately. Each channel strip has its own volume and EQ (where you can alter the treble, mid and bass). Channels may also have a monitor and/or reverb knob.

2. **Main out controls.** These controls affect the sound of the mixer globally, meaning they control the overall volume, monitor, reverb and EQ.

3. **Speaker output section.** This is where you plug in your speakers and monitors. Speakers and monitors are plugged into their designated outputs.

You can get a powered mixer, which means that all the power you need to run it is included in the mixer. Powered mixers use unpowered speakers. If you use an unpowered mixer, you will need a separate power amp or powered speakers.

Mixer.

4. Speakers and Monitors

Speakers are the final step, where the electric signal is converted to actual sound. They must be connected to your powered mixer or power amplifier using speaker cables. Typically, bands use at least two speakers to ensure the music sounds good throughout the room. Speakers are usually mounted on stands so the sound can disperse. The size of the venue and loudness of your band will determine what size speakers you need.

Monitors are a special type of speaker that faces the band so the band members can hear themselves during a performance. Monitors are placed on the floor and are angled upwards toward the musician. For smaller venues, the vocalist may be the only person needing a monitor, but for larger gigs, it is common for each member to have his or her own monitor. Monitors can be mixed to meet individual needs through the mixer. For example, there may be four instrumentalists who have their own monitors, but the guitarist may only wish to hear her guitar and the lead vocalist in her monitor.

PA system.

MICING INSTRUMENTS THROUGH THE PA SYSTEM

For most of your smaller gigs, it probably won't be necessary to mic the instruments in the band. For larger performances, such as corporate events or concerts, it is crucial to use mics, particularly for your guitar amp and the drum kit. You may also want to put a little bit of bass through the PA, particularly if you are trying to get people to dance. If you need lots of bass, you should consider renting *subwoofers* (large speakers designed specifically for bass frequencies), since too much bass may cause your system to distort.

The reason to put instruments through the PA is not only to increase the volume but to create balance throughout the room for the listener. For example, sometimes if your amp is positioned in an awkward place on the stage, only certain people in the audience will hear it, therefore micing the amp (even for a little boost of volume) allows you to be heard all over the room. If you have to put a sax player through the PA, it is best to use a clip-on mic, which attaches itself to the bell (the mouth of the sax where the sound comes out). Most professional sax players own their own clip-on mics and will bring them to their gigs. For micing drums, it's not necessary to mic the whole kit. The snare and the kick drums are traditionally the only parts that are miced, since the vocal mics will pick up the rest of the drums.

Dynamic mics are a good choice for close micing. The mic should be anywhere from one to six inches away from the amp.

If you have a *line out* on your amp (usually situated in the back of the amp), you can plug a guitar cord into it and then plug it into one of the channels of the mixing board. For better results, try placing a mic in front of your amp. You can use a Shure SM57, which is a standard mic for instruments.

Band Tip No. 11—Carrying Your Gear

It's important to be able to carry your own gear around without having to ask for any help from the guys. However, it's not a sign of weakness to ask for help with something difficult, like bringing your amp up a flight of stairs. If you are the person who owns the PA, you should recruit the other band members to carry it in and out of your vehicle, particularly since you are the one providing it.

CARRYING GEAR

Most guitarists start out playing their guitar in the comfort of their own homes, but at some point you will want to start rehearsing and performing with other musicians. One of the challenges that accompanies this is lugging your gear around. You may run into a situation where you are rehearsing or performing a few times a month; you will soon find out how exhausting moving gear around can be. The first challenge is moving the gear out of your house, especially up a flight of stairs. The next challenge is fitting your equipment in a vehicle without damaging your instruments or the vehicle. And the final challenge is getting your gear from the car into the venue. Then, when you are done with the rehearsal or gig, you have to bring everything back home. These tasks can quickly wear you out, particularly if you have no one to help you. Here are some suggestions:

1. **Buy yourself a gig bag rather than a hard case for your guitar.** Gig bags are lightweight and have foam sewn into them for protection. They also come with lots of pockets for accessories like guitar cords, extra straps and music books. Look for gig bags that have extra straps in the back that allow you to carry your guitar like a backpack, freeing up your arms to carry other gear.

2. **Buy a combo amp.** Although owning a head and cabinet is very versatile, it's probably more convenient to own a combo amp. They are much smaller and lighter. Try to get an amp that already has casters (small wheels underneath). If it doesn't have casters, you can buy them at a music store or a hardware store and have them installed.

3. **Lift correctly.** When lifting gear, always put the pressure on your thighs and tilt your pelvis inwards, to avoid straining your lower back (which can put you out of commission).

4. **Use a dolly.** If you have to carry around other gear, like mic stands and a PA system, you will need a dolly (see picture to the right). A *dolly* is a foldable cart that has wheels and can be opened up and laid flat so you can lay all your gear on it. You obviously can't use it to go up and down stairs, but a dolly is extremely handy when you are bringing your gear back and forth from your vehicle. Look for a dolly that is designed specifically for musicians, since it will be much lighter and more compact.

Use a dolly to carry your gear.

GLOSSARY OF TECHNICAL TERMS

Following are some technical terms you may come across while talking or playing with other musicians.

Acoustics—The effect of a room on the sound of music. Rooms can be described as "dead" (having no echo) when they have a lot of absorbing material like drapes and heavy furniture or "live" (having lots of echo) if there are wood floors, bare walls or lots of glass.

Analog—*Analog* signals are continuous variable waves. LPs, cassettes, electric guitars and most amplifiers are examples of analog technology. Analog has the reputation of sounding "natural" but is prone to background noise or "hiss" creeping into the signal.

Decibel (dB)—A unit for measuring loudness.

Digital—*Digital* signals are stored in binary code using 1's and 0's. CDs, MP3s and digital effects processors are examples of digital technology. Digital audio can be copied and edited with no noise or loss of quality. Some musicians who prefer analog claim that digital recordings sound cold or sterile, but advances in technology are gradually eliminating this complaint.

Direct box—A device (small box) placed in the signal chain between an electric guitar (or bass) and a PA system or recording console. If a guitar is plugged into the mixer without a direct box, the signal can sound weak and thin.

Effects loop—A feature found on some guitar amplifiers that consists of an input and output usually labelled "effects send" and "effects return." An effects loop allows some effects (usually time-based effects like a chorus or delay) to interact better with the amplifier instead of going through the regular input.

Feedback—A squealing sound typically caused by a signal that keeps repeating through an amplifier or PA system. This is usually caused by poor microphone placement or too much gain on an amplifier. Rock guitarists sometimes use carefully controlled feedback as a deliberate effect.

Frequency—The number of sound vibrations per second. In relation to sound, frequency corresponds to pitch; for example, lower frequency = lower pitch.

Harmonic—A vibration whose frequency is a multiple of the *fundamental,* or basic frequency, of a note. A musical tone is made up of many *harmonics,* which determine the *timbre,* or tone, of an instrument. A piano can play the exact same note as a guitar, but it will sound different because it has a different set of harmonics.

Hertz (Hz)—A unit of measurement equal to one cycle per second, used to measure frequency. The human ear can generally hear frequencies from 20Hz to 20,000Hz (low frequency to high).

MIDI—(Musical Instrument Digital Interface). The standard digital language that lets electronic instruments, samplers, sequencers, drum machines and keyboards communicate with each other and computers.

Octave—The distance between two notes with the same name. Going up one octave doubles the frequency. For example, if you start at A, whose frequency is 440Hz, then go up one octave, you end up at another A whose pitch is 880Hz.

Ohms—A measure of a speaker cabinet's electrical *impedance* (the amount of strain the speaker places on the amplifier). It is very important to use speaker cabinets that match the recommended impedance for your amplifier. If a guitar amplifier is rated at 8 ohms, you could damage it by attaching a 4 ohm or 16 ohm speaker.

Phase—When *in phase,* two or more sound waves are aligned in harmony with each other and sound good. When *out of phase,* the sound waves are out of sync and there will be a cancellation of certain frequencies, which can cause distortion. It's important to understand this concept if you use multiple speaker cabinets or are in charge of setting up the PA.

Resonance—Resonance occurs when sound causes two items to vibrate in harmony at a given frequency. A typical example would be when a speaker in an amplifier causes its cabinet to resonate. This can sound good or bad depending on the frequency.

Reverb—Reverb is usually a control on an amplifier which can make the guitar sound as if it is in a much larger room. It adds an "echo" to your tone that also tends to soften the sound.

Sample—Taking a recorded sound and reusing it as an instrument or element of a new recording. For example, some recordings use drum samples instead of a real drum kit.

Sequencer—A device used to play, record and arrange MIDI tracks. Sequencers are typically used for backing tracks on a recording or live solo performances.

Wattage—The rating used to specify how much power an amplifier can put out or how much power a speaker can handle. Amplifiers that are 5 to 20 watts are considered practice or recording amplifiers; those that are 30 watts and above are for performing in a live setting.

CHAPTER 3
PERFORMANCE KNOWLEDGE

There are many aspects to being a professional guitarist, such as the ability to perform well on stage. You may not think of performance as something that needs to be studied, but since it is where all of your music study will eventually lead, you will need to spend some time working on it. You may think that you are an artist at heart and your music will speak for itself. Although this is true, in today's competitive market, every skill you can develop is considered a bonus. In this chapter, we will cover some of the aspects that will help you become a skillful performer.

Band Tip No. 12—Bring Your Friends

Always invite friends and family to see your shows. This is a good way to guarantee that you will get some more gigs since the owner of the establishment is making money (that is, if you invite the people who you think will be spending money!). This is a good idea even when you are only filling in for another musician. Not only will the owner of the establishment appreciate it, but so will the leader of the band because you are making him/her look good. This way when they need a guitarist again, you will stand a better chance of getting the call.

PERFORMANCE PREPARATIONS

Before your performance begins, you should prepare yourself so you will be able to focus without too many distractions. Following is a list of suggestions to help you relax and enjoy your gig.

1. **Dress appropriately for the venue.** If you're not certain what the proper apparel is for an event, make sure to ask the leader of the band. If it's your gig, ask whoever booked you if they want casual wear or something a little dressier. You can usually tell by the clientele, but it's always safer to ask. Bring extra shoes if your feet tire easily from standing. You may also want to carry an extra top (something suitable of course) in case you get cold. There's nothing worse than getting stuck under an air vent that makes you feel uncomfortable for a whole night.

2. **Be familiar with all the songs.** You should always make an effort to know all of your songs from memory. Having a music stand is okay in some venues, like for jazz or corporate gigs, but for a concert or festival, it's less professional to have a stand blocking the audience's view. If you're busy reading music, you won't be as focused on your performance. Know your songs inside out; this allows you to focus on your playing. As well, the person who got the gig should make a *set list* for the band (a set list is a sheet of paper that lists the order of songs for each set). It's a lot more professional to follow a set list than to call out the songs. Set lists are just a guide and can be changed if the mood of your audience calls for it.

3. **Warm up before your performance.** You should do vocal and guitar warm-ups before your gig. You can do your vocal warm-ups on the drive over. There are CDs you can buy that are specifically for warm-ups. You can do your guitar warm-ups at the performance after you tune up your instrument. (You should always tune with a tuner at your gigs rather than using your ear. Foot pedal tuners are a handy addition to your other pedals and allow you to tune silently before each set.) You can use a scale and picking exercise, or play a riff that you are having difficulty with. Your warm-ups don't need to be excessive, but the more warmed up you are the more at ease you will feel, particularly for some of the more difficult parts you will need to play.

4. **Be sure your gear is well maintained.** There's nothing more embarrassing than arriving at a gig and realizing that your equipment is not functioning. It can cost you the gig and you will lose respect from your bandmates. Everyone is responsible for his/her own gear; you should be checking your stuff regularly to make sure everything is operational. If you are doing bigger events, concerts or festivals, you may consider bringing an extra guitar in case the unthinkable happens and your main guitar doesn't work. As previously mentioned, bring a small repair kit with extra strings, straps and anything else that may be needed.

5. **Eating and drinking.** This may seem unimportant, but eating the wrong kind of foods can make your performance difficult. Junk food for instance can feel great while you are eating it, but after an hour or so can drain you of all your energy. Eating healthy foods will keep your energy stable and you won't have to worry about feeling like you want to go sleep in a corner somewhere. If there is no food available at the venue, bring some healthy snacks with you. Since many of the venues you will be playing will have alcohol, you may need to know what your limitations are. It's easy to have a few drinks too many before realizing it. Not only can alcohol affect your performance, but you could lose your license, or worse, if you are driving.

6. **Arrive on time.** You should make a habit of leaving yourself extra time to get to your gigs. Arriving late not only stresses *you* out but also the other members of the band. This sort of stress can really affect your playing and bring bad energy to every one else. Generally, you should give yourself half an hour to 45 minutes to set up your guitar and amp plus your driving time. If you are bringing the PA, you will need even more time since you need to unload as well. If someone is helping you with the PA, be sure to set up a mutual arrival time.

Band Tip No. 13—Act Confident and Positive

Never discuss your insecurities or share negative feelings with your bandmates. It only spreads negative energy; and by voicing these feelings, you give your insecurities more power over you. Men rarely talk about their insecurities, especially around their peers, since they know it can be used against them down the road. As women, we tend to be honest and want to share with others what we are feeling. This may make you feel better, but it can affect other people's opinion of your abilities. Eventually, as you gain more experience, your confidence will naturally increase. If you need to speak to someone, share your thoughts with a friend or mentor outside the band.

ASSERTIVE SHOWMANSHIP

Now that you know how to prepare for a gig, you can focus on showmanship techniques. Most of your audience will be non-musicians looking to being entertained. Being proficient as a guitarist will impress your audience because you are a woman. But you shouldn't depend on that; you also need to develop your performance skills. Your audience already considers you a professional (because you are performing in front of them) and they just want to relax and enjoy the show. When you're first starting to perform, it's normal for you to feel nervous. But, believe it or not, your listeners don't need to be aware of this. The adage of "fake it 'till you make it" applies in this situation. If you appear confident, even when you don't feel it, people will assume that you *are* confident. They don't know how long you've been performing so they will take you at face value. Here are some tricks and attitudes you can use to give the impression that you are a seasoned musician.

1. **Relax.** Don't be too hard on yourself. The fact that you are able to land a gig means you have, to a certain extent, already "arrived." Being at ease will also make the rest of the band at ease as well as your audience.

2. **Have fun.** Allow yourself to laugh and put a smile on your face. This will be projected onto your audience. Just remember the reason you got into music was because you really enjoy it, so let that be evident to the people around you.

3. **Don't worry about mistakes.** Everyone makes mistakes, even seasoned musicians. The key is not to bring attention to yourself or to your mistake when it happens. Just keep playing as if nothing happened. This also goes with other members in the band when they make mistakes. No one likes to be singled out, so the best thing to do is just to ignore it. If there are too many mistakes while you're performing, you may need to reevaluate if you need to spend more time on personal rehearsal or band rehearsal.

4. **Stand tall.** It is often said that people who have a straight posture appear more confident. Also be sure to look into your audience and make eye contact with people. After all, you are performing to people, and this small effort makes them feel like you are including them in your experience.

5. **Communicate.** If you are the front person, you should be speaking to your audience, which creates continuity in your sets. You don't need to speak before every tune, but your performance can seem impersonal if you don't add something here and there. Perhaps you can say the name of the next song and who the original performer is. Or you can invite people to get up and dance. If you are selling CDs, let your audience know they can purchase one during your breaks. It doesn't need to be over the top, just be yourself. If you are doing a concert or festival, you may want to practice beforehand what you will say. But for smaller gigs, you can treat it more like a regular conversation. Go visit other bands that have been around awhile and study how they communicate with their audience.

6. **Be friendly.** Take time during your breaks to get to know the people who have been listening to your music. This can be a challenge if you are naturally shy, but sometimes just acknowledging people and asking how they are enjoying their evening is all that is necessary to open up a conversation. Generally, people are intrigued by musicians and honored that you are taking the time to speak to them. You don't need to spend your whole break talking to people, but it always looks good to management if they see you engaging in conversation with their guests.

7. **Showcase yourself.** Don't be afraid to make yourself stand out from the band, especially when you are playing a solo. Men are never afraid to show off their skills, and actually wait for the opportunity to do so. This is how they let their peers know where they stand with their ability. When you are soloing, be confident and make sure the audience can see you.

Photo courtesy of Daisy Rock Guitars

3 Kisses Texas *describe their unique sound as "Texas Party Punk." Formed in 2004, the band is fronted by singer/guitarist Tish Meeks. They are renowned for their high-energy live performances.*

CHAPTER 4
STUDIO KNOWLEDGE

Now that you understand the skills needed to be a performing guitarist, it's time to take a look at a different aspect of playing the guitar: being a studio guitarist. You may desire in the future to do some recording of your own music. This may be for a demo that you are putting together for promotional reasons, or perhaps your original band is deciding to release its first CD. Whatever the reason, you'll need to understand the basics of what it takes to record your guitar.

BEING A STUDIO GUITARIST

Some guitarists, after they have recorded a few times, seem to feel more comfortable in a studio than they do playing live. Although recording and performing guitar have a lot of commonalities, there are some major differences. For example, you may enjoy working with computers, which are an essential part of modern studios. You may have a knack for combining different guitars, effects and amplifiers to create new sounds, which is another great trait to have as a studio guitarist. Or, perhaps, you are not a real "people person" and enjoy the more isolated environment of the studio. These are some of the reasons that guitarists choose a career in the studio over performing live. This doesn't mean that there are guitarists who don't do both successfully, but you may find that you enjoy one over the other and therefore desire to put your efforts where you feel more suited. (For more information on being a studio guitarist, see *The Complete Studio Guitarist* by Vivian Clement; Alfred/National Guitar Workshop #22544.)

You will need to acquire a lot of skill and diversity if you want to be a professional studio guitarist. If you are simply planning to record your own music in your home studio, you still need to know some fundamentals of recording. Let's first take a look at what it takes to be a professional studio guitarist.

Guitarist in the studio.

When it comes to performing live, accuracy in your playing is not as important as when you are recording. The studio requires more discipline in your technique and skill since whatever you play, including sloppy technique, is recorded. Below is a list of requirements for working in a professional studio environment.

TIPS FOR BEING A STUDIO GUITARIST

1. **Lots of different equipment.** You should have electric guitars (hollow body and solid body with single- and double-coil pickups), acoustic and classical guitars, a few different amplifiers and/or amp simulators (to emulate all available sounds) and lots of guitar effects. You may not start out with all this equipment at first, but eventually you should acquire all or most of these items.

2. **Great sight-reading skills.** Sight-reading is the ability to read music you have never seen before on the spot; this includes note reading and chord reading.

3. **Knowledge of lots of chords.** This would include a lot of extended chords.

4. **Ability to work under pressure.** A lot of times you may be waiting for your turn to record your part, but when it is your time to record you must be able to record quickly and accurately without having to re-record too many times because of mistakes.

5. **Ability to follow instructions.** Most of the time you'll be working with the producer and/or the artist whose music is being recorded. You may not always agree with what they're wanting you to record, therefore you need to be able to follow orders easily without taking things personally.

6. **Punctuality.** Since a studio charges by the hour, it is crucial that you always be on time for a session. You should also be prepared to stay longer when necessary.

7. **Be able to play a lot of different genres of music.** You will need to know a lot of different types of music in order to be a successful studio guitarist.

8. **Be a great improviser.** As well as knowing a lot of different genres of music, you will need to be proficient at soloing over many styles of music.

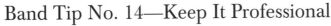

Band Tip No. 14—Keep It Professional

You don't need to like everyone in the band in order to work with them. This is difficult for women who tend to feel two-faced if they have to hang around with someone they dislike. With men, they know that a team is made up of many different people and don't feel they need to get along with everyone to belong to the team. If you are having a personality clash with someone in a band, you can be friendly without building a friendship. Just be professional and courteous with them.

SETTING UP YOUR HOME STUDIO

As you can see, being a studio guitarist can be quite an undertaking. That does not mean you can't enjoy doing some recording on your own. More and more, guitarists are finding that owning a home studio is not only rewarding but quite feasible. Gone are the days when you had to invest tens of thousands of dollars to own a decent studio. With just a few thousand dollars or less, you will find that you can accomplish quite a bit with some of the new technologies that are on the market today.

The best approach to take for setting up your studio is to go down to your local music store and find out what they presently have available. There are many products to choose from. Decide first of all what you will be using it for, this way you won't buy something too complex for your needs. Will you be recording just yourself and your guitar, or will you be recording a few instruments as well? Let the salespeople know your goals so they can show you the right gear. (Keep in mind that most music stores have monthly payment plans which makes setting up your studio more affordable.) You can also use your present computer and buy designated software to do all of your recording; this is a little more complex, and you will need to have a computer that has a lot of RAM (computer memory).

Stand-alone recording devices are very popular because they have all the necessary components for recording built-in. All you need to do to get started is plug in your guitar and mic.

Stand-alone recording devices.

If you are in a band, get some of the other members to lend a hand in putting your studio together. They may have some friends who already have a studio and would be willing to assist. Or, you can barter your services by having everyone pitch in for the equipment and you will be the one to do the recordings and provide the space.

TIPS FOR THE HOME STUDIO

1. You will need a room or section of a room with adequate lighting and telephone hookup (if you are using a computer to connect to the Internet). A desk or table placed near an electrical outlet and power strip (if you need several outlets). If you don't already have speakers, you will need to buy some. Look for speakers that are more like studio monitors. These monitors have a flat response (no EQ added to them). It's important to buy good quality monitors, otherwise it will be next to impossible to tell what quality of sound you are actually getting.

2. You will also need a stand-alone workstation. If you are using a computer, it should be fast and have sufficient RAM with designated recording software. A soundcard is also necessary. Your computer will already have a soundcard, but you will need to upgrade it to accommodate your recording projects. You will also need a MIDI (Musical Instrument Digital Interface) interface if you want to record keyboards. Plug-ins are also software based effects (like EQ and reverb) that are used to enhance the sound of your recording. Some already come with your recording software. If not, you can purchase them.

3. Be sure to get a half-decent microphone if you are recording vocals. A vocal that has been recorded on a cheap microphone cannot be made to sound great, no matter how many effects you put on it. You don't need to invest a lot of money on a mic and you can even look for a second-hand one. This is one place where you don't want to be too frugal. Be sure to purchase a mic that is used for vocals and not for instruments, since they both produce different results. A salesperson at a music store will be able to assist you with this. Typically, a condenser mic is better suited for studio use than a dynamic mic.

4. Check the Internet to find out what software and plug-in effects are available. You may find many of them are free. Also, check out sites that will give you tips on setting up your studio.

5. Read trade magazines that are specifically geared to home studio musicians. Magazines are a great source of valuable information and keep you in the loop on what is new in the market.

As you can see, there is a lot of information when it comes to recording your guitar. Rather than being overwhelmed, you can view this as an area for future exploration when you feel ready.

Part 2:
Minding Your Own Business

CHAPTER 5
BUSINESS 101

SETTING UP YOUR BUSINESS

When you begin playing for money, you will probably want to set yourself up as a business. This is done mainly so you can write off different parts of your business on your taxes. Like it or not, some of the money you make from your gigs will be required to be sent to the government. You may feel that since most of your gigs are cash, and there is no paper trail, you don't need to claim your earnings. However, you will quickly discover that evading taxes is not a good idea. Aside from the fact that this is illegal and comes with severe penalties if you ever get caught, you can never build up your credit. To get loans (for gear, or in the future a house or car) you will need to show that you are a responsible citizen and able to pay back any money you borrow. Financial institutions are hesitant to lend money to people who don't appear to be making an income.

To set yourself up as a business you need to pay a visit to your local government office (or check to see if it can be done online). For a small fee (costs vary according to where you live), you can register your name as a business. You will then be given documentation proving that you are now a business. What you will want to do from that point on is to keep any receipts that have to do with your music business. Some or all of your purchases can be written off on your taxes. There are many other business-related deductions such as travel and home office expenses. You will need to keep all of your receipts and file them in an organized fashion. At the end of the year, you can bring your receipts to an accounting firm and they will help you file these deductions properly.

There are many books covering this topic that you can find at your local bookstores or online, or check out the web under "how to set up a business." You may also have a friend who owns a business who will be willing to show you the ropes. The best thing is to know the basics and set up your business right so you won't run into problems with the tax department later down the road.

Photo courtesy of Mark Harlan/Star File Photo, Inc.

Jewel Kilcher (b. 1974), better known to the world simply as Jewel, is famous for her crystalline vocals and folk guitar style. After years of "paying her dues," Jewel burst onto the music scene with her 1995 hit "You Were Meant for Me."

BOOKING GIGS

If you have never booked your band before, looking for gigs can seem quite daunting. One thing to keep in mind when you are out scouting for places to play is that you need to have a good promotional kit to leave with any bar owners who may be interested (see page 55).

One way to locate bars that have bands is to find the listings in your local newspaper. Most cities have an entertainment section where they list the venues with live entertainment and also list who is playing. Look on the web and type in your city and live entertainment to see what turns up. Pay attention to what types of bands the bars are hiring. If a certain venue has only country bands and you play alternative rock there is no point in wasting your time or a promo kit trying to get a gig there. Sometimes, you can convince an owner to try something different, but chances are most of the clientele will be expecting to hear what they are used to.

Look for venues that play similar music to yours. Once you have located several places you would like to perform at, go check them out on a night when a band is playing. If you feel your music would suit the venue, you can then ask to speak to the person who books the bands. This will often be the owner or manager, but at times it may be the bartender or another employee. Whoever it is will likely want a promo kit, so be sure to have one handy.

When you first start playing, people looking to hire you will want to know where you have performed. If you don't have much experience, it may be a challenge to get into the scene. A good way to gain experience is to start playing anywhere you can, like a friend's party, your school or a community center. Of course the law may require that you be of legal drinking age, therefore you should also look to play in places that are for all ages. You should try to gain as much experience as possible before attempting to perform in bars, since you will be expected to be professional in all aspects. The more opportunities you have to play beforehand will be helpful in preparing you for bars later on.

ORIGINAL VS. COVER BAND

Many musicians start their careers playing in their own original band before going on to play in a *cover band,* or band that plays music written by other artists. This is often a good way to start, since you will gain a lot of experience. Most places that you play original music will expect you to bring your own crowd. Many times you will only make money if you sell tickets ahead of time or charge a cover at the door. You will also be able to sell your CDs if you have any.

If you decide to work as a cover band, you will be expected to play mostly songs that people are familiar with and want to dance to. Some places don't mind a few original songs and will allow you to sell your CDs as well. The best thing to do is to ask the owner what is expected.

BOOKING MUSICIANS

As you progress in your musical career, you will encounter many musicians along the way. Start collecting business cards for future reference. You never know when a situation will arise where one of your band members is unable to perform and you will need someone to fill in for the night. This pertains mostly to a cover band rather than an original band, since original music usually takes many rehearsals before the band is ready to perform live. There are many musicians who are a part of a few bands and also work as subs (or substitutes, musicians who work with several bands at the same time, also called "jobbers").

If you live in a busy city where the music scene is vibrant, the better musicians will usually be gigging, but they may be available for an evening. As well, if you know ahead of time that you will be needing someone because one of your members won't be available, you can call up your list of players to see who is available. Most jobber musicians know a lot of songs, but some will ask if you have charts. If you don't have charts, you will need to choose songs for the night that are very popular. You can send your sub a song list (along with the keys the tunes are in) so he/she can tell you if they know most of the tunes. A jobbing musician will often take the gig and pick up some of the tunes they don't know off the internet. Usually they are good enough to figure out the tunes on their own or may ask you at the gig to go over some of the songs they are unfamiliar with. It's best to ask ahead of time how familiar they are with your song list.

Band Tip No. 15—Don't Sell Yourself Short

You should never undercharge for your services as a band. Some young musicians do this so they can encourage a bar owner to hire them instead of another seasoned band that charges more. This is a big mistake, since at some point you will become that seasoned musician. When bands undercut other bands or work for free they are affecting their own future earnings. Bar owners would love to pay as little as possible for their bands, and this sort of practice damages the entire industry.

DEALING WITH MONEY

If you are the leader of the band, you will be the one handling the money and paying your musicians. When you first book the band at a venue, you can ask the owner how much he/she pays and if it is cash or check. You should never feel intimidated asking about money. This is a part of business and a bar owner expects you to be able to deal professionally with the subject. You should already have a good idea from other bands what the going rate is for your area. At the end of the night, if the person who books you has left, you can simply ask the bartender who you would speak with to get paid. If you get paid by check, you should have checks from your own account to pay each of the band members. You don't need to open up a business account, since this costs extra money. You can simply use your own personal account.

If you are the one booking gigs for the band, and bringing the sound system, you may want to try to get a *leader's fee*. This could be anywhere from $25–$100 more than anyone else in the band. Sometimes you can negotiate a few extra dollars from an owner. For the most part, many professional musicians have no problem with the leader making a little more money for her efforts.

Band Tip No. 16—Impress the Agent

If you invite an agent to see your band perform, make certain you are well-rehearsed and have your show up to speed. Good agents are very busy; if they actually do come to see your show and you still need to work out the kinks, they will not be impressed. You usually don't get a second chance to make a first impression.

DEALING WITH AGENTS

To get into some of the rooms you would like to play, or to start doing corporate events, you may have to work with an agent. You can get the name and number of the agents by contacting the venue where you wish to perform. If you are trying to perform for a certain company, you can call that company to inquire about who is responsible for booking entertainment for their special events.

Agents for your area are also listed in the Yellow Pages and on the Internet. Many times an agent will want to see you perform, so you can tell him the other venues at which you are playing and he can come check you out. Agents usually get 10%–20% of what you make and don't always have a great reputation for honesty, so you will need to be street-smart when working with them. They often have a roster of musicians that they already represent so you will need to be professional and convince them that they should work with you.

Photo courtesy of Al Pereira/Star File Photo, Inc.

Tracy Chapman (b. 1964) helped revive the folk genre in the late 1980s. She burst onto the scene in 1988 with the top 10 hit "Fast Car." In 1997, Chapman won the Best Rock Song Grammy for "Give Me One Reason." She is an accomplished singer, songwriter, guitarist and political activist.

PERFORMANCE CONTRACT

Some performances you do will require a contract. It's a good idea for a bigger show where you are making a considerable amount of money that you request a 50% deposit (which they can send by mail in the form of a check). This way if the other party cancels, you can still pay the band for the night that they lost a gig. You can inform whoever is hiring you that your policy is to get a deposit and that you will be faxing or emailing them a contract for the event. You can also alter or add conditions that may be specific to that particular event. Below is an example of a contract.

CONTRACT # _____   LIVE PERFORMANCE CONTRACT

> **CONTRACT AND ANY APPLICABLE DEPOSIT MUST BE RECEIVED BY THE DATE(S) SPECIFIED BELOW OR ARTIST HAS THE RIGHT TO VOID CONTRACT**

This contract is for the personal services of musicians on the date of engagement described below between the undersigned purchaser of music (herein after called "purchaser") and the undersigned musician or musicians is made this _____ day of the month of _____ in the year_____.

Place of engagement: _____
Address: _____
_____

Artist/Act: _____
Other Artist/Act: _____

Date of engagement: _____   Guaranteed agreed upon: _____
Time of engagement: _____
Length of Show: _____
Type of engagement: _____   Contracts due: _____
Seating capacity: _____   Deposit of: _____
Ticket scale 1: _____   Deposit due: _____
Ticket scale 2: _____   Balance due: _____
Ticket scale 3: _____   GST (6%): _____
Ticket scale 4: _____   Balance amount: _____
Gross potential: _____   Balance due prior to performance: _____
                                              Artist percentage: _____ %
                                              Purchaser percentage: _____ %

Sound and lights provided by: _____

***** ARTIST RIDER(S) ATTACHED HERETO IS MADE A PART HEREOF*****

IN WITNESS WHEREOF, THE PARTIES HERETO HAVE HEREUNTO SET THEIR NAMES AND SEALS ON THE DAY AND YEAR FIRST ABOVE WRITTEN

Purchaser: _____
Address: _____
_____

Contact: _____
Phone: _____   Fax: _____

_____   _____
SIGNATURE OF PURCHASER OR AGENT   SIGNATURE OF SIGNATORY MUSICIAN

Payment can be made to The Female Guitar Band

WRITING PROFESSIONAL LETTERS

Whenever sending out your promo kit, you'll need to include a letter. Learning to write professional letters is a must. It is important that you present yourself as professionally as possible since it is expected in this industry. When typing a letter, make sure you spell the name of the person you are contacting correctly. If you are unsure of any information, contact their office and request the proper spelling as well as address. Keep your letters brief and to the point, but don't be afraid to be specific on exactly what you are asking. You should always include some of your recent accomplishments. (Having your own logo—which may coincide with your business name—is also a good idea.) Always follow up with a phone call, a few weeks after you send your kit, to see if it was received and feel out if there is any interest in hiring you. Below is a sample letter.

August 10th, 2007

Mr. John Agent
123 Musicville Street
Anytown, Florida
USA

Dear Mr. Agent,

Enclosed please find my promotional package, which you requested in our previous conversation.

My band, "The Female Guitar Band," has been performing in Anytown and surrounding areas for several years. We have two CDs that have been receiving radio airplay through College Radio FM680 and we have won three Battles of the Bands this past year. We are hoping to perform at Mosquito Lounge, for which I understand you are presently the booking agent.

You are invited to come see us live. For a full listing of up and coming performances, check out our website: femaleguitarband.com. I will be contacting you within the next week.

Sincerely

Joan String
555-888-9999
www.femaleguitarband.com

Band Tip No. 17—Invite Others to Sit In

If another musician is in the audience, ask if they would like to do a tune with the band (as long as it's not a problem with the owner or bandleader). Of course, you want to be sure they are qualified to play on your level. This is a good way to network and use it as a bartering opportunity. If you are trying to get your name out there in the music biz, you can always show up at one of their gigs and do a song with their band. This is just another way to promote yourself.

NEGOTIATION SKILLS

Being a good negotiator is an important skill in any business. Not everything in this business is written in stone; there are some situations when you're dealing with owners or agents that you will be able to negotiate. For instance, if you are performing at a corporate event, you should be able to negotiate a deal in which the band gets to eat as well. If the person booking the event says that this is not customary you could explain that this is a part of your policy, and that it's difficult for the band to perform if they haven't been able to eat. If there is still some resistance you could then request one of your breaks to be a little longer so the band would be able to go somewhere and get some food.

Another example of negotiating would be if you are performing somewhere but the fee is a little lower than you normally get for your band. If they are unwilling to pay you more, you could then ask for the hours to be a little shorter; for instance, instead of playing for four hours you will play for three and a half hours. You could also suggest that if you are able to bring a certain number of people to the gig, then you would get paid a higher amount.

You may also have to negotiate with a bandleader who has hired you for gigs. Let's say you have been given 10 gigs to do, but are expected to attend a rehearsal once a week. If you are unwilling to rehearse this much you could work out a situation where you would attend half of the rehearsals but guarantee that you will know all of the music when you do rehearse.

When negotiating, it is important to remember not to feel intimidated by someone else's position. Even though you should always show respect and be professional in business dealings, you also want to make sure that your needs and the needs of your band are being met. Most establishment owners are fairly flexible. However, if your demands are not being met, you will have to decide if you still want to play at that venue. It takes experience to feel confident when negotiating but it is an important skill that you will be able to develop over time. Always keep the other person's point of view in mind. As a business owner their main objective is profit, and as long as they're making money they usually won't have a problem meeting some of your requests. But when business is down, it's not a good idea to get too demanding.

CHAPTER 6
PROMOTING YOURSELF

Band Tip No. 18—Toot Your Own Horn

Most women view self-promotion as bragging, but for men it is the way they let each other know where they stand in the status totem pole. It also gives them an opportunity to find out what their colleagues have been up to. Men look for opportunities to insert their most recent accomplishments into conversations with their buddies. But you may want to be a little more conservative when approaching women who may still view self-promotion as distasteful.

Whether you like it or not, to advance as a professional guitarist, you will need to learn how to promote yourself. Self-promotion is not something women generally feel very comfortable with, since we have been conditioned from a young age that promoting our gifts is unacceptable behavior. However, in the competitive world of the music business, this trait will keep you from moving on to where you perhaps deserve to be. Men, on the other hand, have no problem at all with self-promotion and actually spend most of their time when they are around their colleagues promoting themselves in one way or another. Any time you hear a male musician discussing who he's recently performed with, new gear he has purchased, or some new lick he has learned, he is in effect promoting himself. This is behavior that you should also adopt to demonstrate that you also are going places.

The trick when tooting your horn is to do it subtly, kind of like it's part of the conversation. A suggestion would be to rehearse your accomplishments beforehand, so you can learn to self-promote in a natural manner. It's also a good idea to observe your male musician friends to see how they go about self-promoting and how their colleagues respond to it. In effect, what you are trying to do is leave an impression with other musicians, who will at some point mention your name to other musicians. You are trying to build a reputation in your city as a competent guitarist. Also, make yourself visible at events that are taking place in your area. Some of these events could be trade shows, open mics, etc. Check out area bands when you know there will be other musicians attending. The more visibility you have as a guitarist, the more opportunities will present themselves to you.

Chrissie Hynde (b. 1951) is one of rock's most respected female singer/songwriter/ guitarists. She is best known as the leader and co-founder of the Pretenders, who had a huge influence in the punk/new wave scene of the late 1970s and early '80s.

Photo by Elena Sileo

CREATING YOUR PROMOTIONAL PACKAGE

The first thing you'll need to do to promote yourself is to put together a professional promotional package (also called *promo kit*), which you will send out to booking agents or even record companies. Although a lot of promotion can be done over the Internet via your website, it's still a good idea to have a traditional promotional package. If you are a solo guitarist, the promotional package will be mainly about yourself. If you are with a band, the promotional package will be about the band, but try to get a few shots of yourself with your guitar so you can use these pictures for other opportunities that arise.

Your promo kit is put into a folder and consists of the following:

1. Letter with your logo
2. Business card
3. 8x10 picture with your instrument (can be in color or black-and-white)
4. Biography
5. Press clippings*
6. Fact sheet*
7. CD or demo
8. Press release
9. Poster*

* Not always necessary for bars and smaller venues.

Each component should have your contact information in case it is separated from the rest of the material. Let's look at each one separately.

1. **Letter.** As mentioned on page 52, your letterhead should feature your logo. Be brief and state your purpose for sending the package. The paper that your letter is on should be of good quality. Never forget to do a spell check.

2. **Business card.** Be sure to include a professional business card. People tend to keep business cards for a long time. Don't make your business card too sterile. This is the music business so you can have some fun with it.

3. **8x10 picture.** An 8x10 picture is standard in a promo kit. You will want to get a professional photographer to take this picture. They are easy to locate through your Yellow Pages or the Internet. Never use a picture that you have taken yourself, unless you are familiar with photography. Professional photographers know how to use lighting to bring out your best features. This will usually run you a few hundred bucks, but you can't afford not to have this done professionally. If it is a band shot, everyone can pitch in, and be sure to get a few shots of you alone with your guitar. To get some ideas, look inside magazines for some interesting pictures and bring them with you to the shoot. A promo picture is a more traditional one, rather than too creative, which is what you may use for your poster or CD. You can also get a white border at the bottom where you can put yours or your band's name; this picture can then be used by bar owners to promote upcoming shows. While you are getting your 8x10 shot, you can also get the rest of your pictures for your CD and poster. You should check out a few photographer's and try to find one who has done band shots before. Ask to see their portfolio. Ask other musicians who they used as a photographer. Sometimes the photographer's name appears on CDs or posters so you can contact them if you see someone's picture that you like. When you get your pictures done, you can ask for proofs, which are simply prints of your pictures. Or, you can ask to have the pictures on CD; this way you will have them in digital format, which is a lot more cost effective than buying individual prints from the photographer. You can also use the pictures on the CD for your website or for your letterhead and business card. There is software available that allows you to manipulate photos and make them more artsy.

4. **Biography.** Your biography is a one-page description of your musical history. People are interested in your background and reasons for getting into music. It can state some of your earlier accomplishments as well as what you have done recently. For instance, perhaps you won a music award of some type, or you studied under a famous teacher. You can also list your CDs and give the address for your website.

5. **Press clippings.** This includes anything published in the media about you or your band. It could be a newspaper clipping or an article in a magazine. As you learn how to get press for yourself, you will want to include it in your promo kit as well as on your website. Keep your original clippings and photocopy a bunch of them so that you can file them for future use.

6. **Fact sheet.** This sheet includes basic information about yourself or your band; for instance, when your band started playing. You will also want to list all the members of the band, your accomplishments and what genre of music you perform. Also, list all the places at which you have performed and any information about present or upcoming CDs.

7. **CD or demo.** A press kit is not complete without a CD or a demo of some type. If you presently can't afford to put together a CD, you absolutely need to get a demo of the material you are presently working on. Not only does a CD go into your promo package, you can use it to give to bar owners. You'll also want to have samples of your music on your website for people to download so they can hear what your music is all about.

8. **Press release.** A press release is an announcement sent to the news media and other publications to let the public know what you are presently doing. It should answer the questions "who? what? where? when? and how?" You can also include a quote that someone has made about you. If you are listing performances, make sure to include the dates and times. Mention any awards you have won or other important things you have done. Each paragraph should be no longer than three to four sentences.

9. **Poster.** Some of the pictures you had the photographer take can be used to create a poster. Posters are great for bigger events like festivals. Since they are more costly than regular 8x10 pictures, you won't want to use them in bars. Make sure (if you aren't good with graphics) that you get a graphic designer to make a great poster for you. Today's standards are very high, and people judge you by the graphics that you present to them. This also goes for any other images you present to the public. You can't afford not to have top quality graphics of yourself; they are one of the hallmarks of a professional.

Following are examples of promo kits. These are usually presented in a folder with the picture on the left-hand side, the CD in the sleeve and the rest of the information on the right-hand side.

Promo Kit—Example No. 1

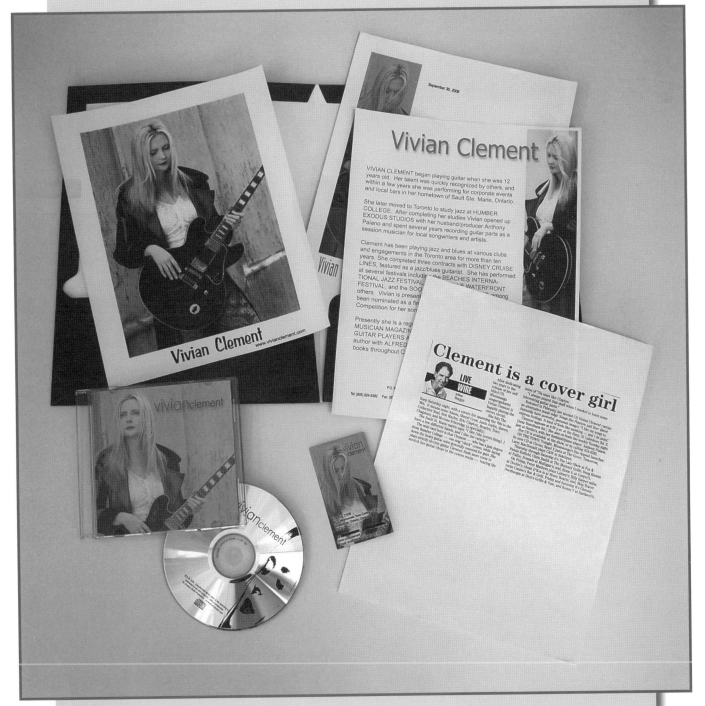

BUILDING CREDENTIALS

Credentials are accomplishments you have accumulated over the years and are a vital part of your success. They give you the necessary notoriety to move ahead on your path of success. Press from your hometown, an award you won for musical competency or certificates of honor in a musical field can all be considered "credentials." A good place to start is where you are right now. Perhaps you've done some teaching at a school, and you've won an award. Be sure to keep the certificate and hang it in your studio where you practice. When people comment on it, you will have the opportunity to talk about your accomplishment. You should also include any accomplishments in your promotional kit.

The following is a list of things you might try to accomplish to add to your credentials as you progress in your career. This information should then be included in your press release, biography or letter.

1. If you are still in school, try to participate in any musical events by yourself or with your band. For example, you could enter a "Battle of the Bands."

2. Volunteer at musical events where you can be part of the team behind the scenes, perhaps the person who collects the tickets at the door or a member of the panel that chooses the bands. This is a great experience to see what people on the other side of the music business are looking for in talent.

3. Once you've been playing guitar for several years, you may decide to teach beginners. This may open the door to other opportunities in the future like teaching at summer camps, which is a great way to network with other musicians who also teach.

4. Start your own guitar clinic in your area. You could offer to do it at a local music store. Make a deal with the owner that if they promote you to their clients and students, you will offer a clinic for free or for a nominal fee. This way the next time you do a clinic you could do it elsewhere, and since you will then have past experience, you can ask for better money.

5. Write an article and put it on your website. You can send it to people on your mailing list that have similar interests as you. This allows people to view you as an expert in the field that you are talking about.

You may not be able to do all the above at the present time. The goal is to build a lot of musical accomplishments (which don't necessarily need to be performance related). For more great ideas pick up the book *101 Ways to Promote Yourself* by Raleigh Pinskey.

Band Tip No. 19—Lend a Hand

If you aren't the one bringing the PA for the band, always be sure to lend a hand bringing in gear. It is always appreciated when other musicians help out. Men usually don't expect women to help out with gear, so when you do, you will gain some brownie points. It also breaks some of the stereotypical attitudes that prevail.

GETTING FREE PRESS

It's not as difficult as you think to get free press, particularly if you are in an area that has a local newspaper or a college paper. Journalists and media personalities are always looking for good stories. Not only is their job to write a column in the newspaper (or in the case of college radio, put together a music program), they need to continually come up with new and interesting features and segments. This provides an opportunity for you to get some free press.

To get into your local newspaper, all you need to do is find out who the columnist is for the entertainment section. Give them a call—introduce yourself and the project you are presently working on, and ask them if you would be able to get a write up of yourself or your band in one of their upcoming columns.

The key to getting press is to offer something that is newsworthy. In other words, you need to be doing something that's a little bit different than any other band that's out there. For instance, you could offer to play for free at a charity event, then contact the newspaper to tell them that you will be there and ask if someone will come to cover that event. This is commonly called *co-marketing,* where one person, or group, partners with another person or group to create a situation with mutual benefits. In this instance, you would be offering free music to the charity organization, and they would be giving you a platform to perform where you can both get free press. There are no limits to creating interesting topics that would attract a newspaper columnist. Another idea would be to host a clinic at a local college, teaching beginning guitar to college students. You could then ask the college newspaper to cover your event in their next printing.

The sky is the limit when it comes to ideas that are interesting and would attract attention from media. Anything you can do that's a little bit different increases your exposure to the general public, which further promotes your career. Although this is a little bit of extra work on your part, the contacts that you make and experience that you gain will be of great benefit in the future. (Always put in that extra 10% of effort; it will only increase your chances of success.)

CREATING A WEBSITE

Having your own website is essential in the music business today. Many artists use their website as an electronic promo kit; often, you can refer people to your website rather than sending your kit the traditional way. Your website should feature the same information as your promotional package, including bio, press clippings, etc. Also, instead of only being able to offer a poster or 8x10, you can have an entire gallery of photographs—of yourself in the studio as well as performing live. If you have a CD, you can inform people as to where they can buy it and even provide links to websites where they can purchase it online. Make a section featuring "snippets" of your CD so people can hear your music. This applies if you have original music that has already been recorded, since you can't record other artists' music without their permission.

You can let your fans know about upcoming gigs. Make a mailing list of friends and fans and email them about any upcoming events. Always keep your website up-to-date and have someone review it for errors or items you might've missed along the way.

It may cost a lot of money to have a professional develop your website, but there are many books available about how you can do this yourself. If you aren't that great on the computer, you can always ask a friend to help you. Another great idea is to dedicate part of your site to teaching guitar. This is yet another way to build credentials. (Of course, you need to be able to offer something that is of value and would be considered somewhat intermediate or advanced). You can also include links to other sites of interest, or request other sites to feature a link to yours.

MySpace.com is another great way to promote yourself, and it's free. It's a wonderful way to network with people from all over the world. You can upload some of your recorded music and invite people to comment on it. You can also add pictures. Having your own website and using sites like MySpace are powerful ways of promoting yourself.

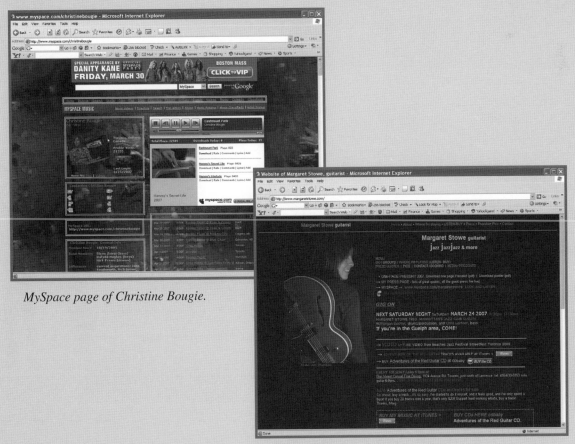

MySpace page of Christine Bougie.

Website of Margaret Stowe.

CHAPTER 7
THE POWER OF NETWORKING

Gone are the days when you could sit at home and have opportunities knock on your door because you had great talent. The guitarists who want to have a promising future in the music biz will be the ones who have learned the amazing influence that *networking* has to offer. What exactly is networking? Networking is meeting people of like mind and interests and building relationships. Over time, these relationships will create opportunities that would not otherwise exist.

Many musicians are under the false impression that because they are ultra-talented, opportunities will find them. In today's market, however, opportunities are often given to people just because they have the right connections. This is nothing new. We've all heard the saying that "it's *who* you know" that counts. This is even truer today. Networking is a skill as old as civilization and has often been the way to success. Talent may open some doors, but these doors are also open to other musicians who are vying for the same breakthroughs. Building lasting relationships through networking is the only way to secure your place amongst the people who are going places.

Not all people you meet will be beneficial to your career. You will find that some are willing to help you and others are not. Because you are a woman, you may also find that some men can act a little inappropriately. There are environments where this is more likely to happen than others, like at a bar where someone may have had a little too much to drink. You should always remain professional, and if a person persists in their inappropriate behavior, it's your cue to leave their presence. You will find that someone worth building a relationship with will first and foremost be open to what your goals are, and most importantly, treat you with respect. Networking with these types of people should be your aim.

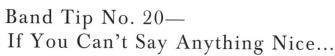

Band Tip No. 20—
If You Can't Say Anything Nice...

Never speak badly about other musicians. The music biz is a small community and things have a way of getting around. It's always best to keep your opinions to yourself. If some musician is a real problem, it won't be long before others figure it out for themselves.

ASSOCIATIONS

Belonging to associations and various groups around your city is a great place to start networking. For instance, if there is a songwriters' association in your area, you may want to attend. This is a good way to meet singer/songwriters who often look for other musicians to play on their demos or CDs. Not all songwriters are great vocalists or have great abilities on an instrument. They are often looking for someone with whom they can start a project.

MUSIC STORES

Music stores are also a good location to meet other musicians. Get to know the staff since they are always in contact with other musicians looking to make things happen. If you are looking for someone to work with, ask the staff to keep an eye out for you in case they come across someone who fits the bill. Also, if you enjoy working in retail, music stores are a phenomenal place to get an overall feel for what goes on in the music field. Apart from bars, they are the place where all musicians must go at some point to buy new gear.

TRADE SHOWS

Many larger cities hold trade shows once or twice a year. Trade shows are usually held in some kind of convention center where retail stores display all the new gear and gadgets that have recently come out on the market. Trade shows usually last a few days, and there is usually an entrance fee (which you can write off from your taxes if you save your receipt). Merchants from surrounding areas and smaller towns come to trade shows to purchase new products for their own stores back home. Even though many trade shows are geared towards retailers, you will always find a slew of musicians who come to the show to check out what's going on. It's a good place to reconnect with musicians you may not have seen for a while and let them know what you have been up to. If you happen to know that one of your local music stores will have a booth at the show, attending will show your support and give you an opportunity to deepen your relationship with them.

Since there is a wide variety of booths on display, you will find opportunities to meet all types of people who may not be musicians but are involved in the music business. For instance, your local radio station might be there, or a music newspaper or magazine. If you are someone who would like to get into writing music articles, this would be a good place to connect. Many experienced people are more than happy to share their stories, and if you let people know what your interests are they may be willing to give you some advice. Of course, you'll want to be sensitive to their time since they are also working and trying to do business. You can ask whoever you meet for their business card, in case you want to speak to them at a future date; and be sure to have lots of your own business cards handy as well.

Band Tip No. 21—Play to Your Strengths

When preparing to play at a jam night, always select a simple, popular song you are sure the band will know. Make sure it's a song you know by heart and can perform very well. It's better to do a simple song that you perform perfectly, than a great song that you perform poorly.

BARS AND JAM NIGHTS

Assuming that you are of the right age to drink, networking at bars can be very effective. You will find that a lot of musicians attend performances of bands with great reputations. Many musicians want to see what their buddies are up to and also go there to network and bump into friends they may not have seen in a while. Busy musicians don't see their colleagues too often since everyone usually gigs at the same time, so performances make a great place to hang out and meet with old friends.

Bars are a place where single people go to meet others. This can get a little tricky, particularly if you are trying to build strictly business relationships with men. It's probably a good idea to come in with another musician friend so you won't feel like a target. If you happen to see someone in the crowd that you would like to meet, maybe a mutual friend or acquaintance can introduce you. If not, you can always look for an opportunity to go and introduce yourself. For instance, let's say there is a guitarist in the crowd from whom you would like to take some lessons. You could introduce yourself by saying you have seen him perform at such and such place and really liked his playing. You could then ask if he would be willing to teach you some of the techniques that he knows. Even if he declines, you may have an opportunity to talk some more and build some kind of relationship. You can always leave your card and tell him that if he ever gets into teaching, you would be interested in taking some lessons.

Jam nights provide a great way to meet other musicians and show off your skills. A jam night is usually held at a bar and there is often a band that hosts the event. Musicians put their names up on a board and are called to come up and play with the band. If you are just starting out as a guitarist and don't have much experience, going to jams will help you, but be sure to choose a jam night that has a lot of beginners so you won't feel too out of your league. Don't forget to bring a tuner. Nothing is more unprofessional than a badly tuned guitar at a jam night. No matter how great you perform, people will not take you seriously if you are out of tune.

FOLLOW-UPS AND REFERRALS

Whenever you go out and network, you will probably come home with a whole bunch of business cards. Stationery stores sell systems to store and organize business cards, so be sure to purchase one of these. Write on the business card where you met the person and some memorable thing about them. It's common to find forgotten business cards in your purse and have no clue who the person is. The reason you should keep business cards is that you never know when you may need to speak to that person again. Sometimes it may even be a few years down the road when you run into a situation where that person may be helpful to you. Even if the person doesn't remember you when you call (sometimes people say they remember even when they don't), they still may be able to help you.

GETTING REFERRALS

Often, you may find that the person with whom you connect is not really the person who can help you out. For example, let's say you went to a trade show and were talking to a guy who fixes amplifiers. Your amp needs to be fixed, so you call him up only to discover that he is so busy he won't be able to help you for at least a few weeks. Since you need your amp for a gig next week, you can ask him if there is anyone he can refer you to. Chances are that he will be able to give you a few numbers of some people who are just as qualified but not as busy. Or, perhaps you met a great bass player who is interested in joining your band, but he later changes his mind for one reason or another. Since he has an idea of what you are looking for, he may be able to give you a few numbers of some other bassists that would be interested.

Referrals are a wonderful way to have doors open up for you. That is why you should never hesitate to meet people. Everybody knows somebody, and even though the person with whom you are speaking can't help you, they most likely know someone else who can. Also, the more people you meet, the more chances *you* will have of being referred when there is a need for someone with your qualifications. For more information on referrals, check out *Drumming up Referrals* by Dan Bodanis.

Band Tip No. 22—Don't Be Sorry

Get out of the habit of always saying "sorry" and apologizing for your opinions. You have a right to be heard and your opinion counts even if no one else agrees with you. Men rarely apologize, even when they're wrong.

Part 3: Successful Female Attitudes

CHAPTER 8
20 COMMON MISTAKES WOMEN MAKE

So far, we've examined the importance of musical, technical and performance knowledge. We've also taken a look at the need to be familiar with different aspects of business. Part 3 will be dedicated to the attitudes that are necessary when working with men in the music business.

The feminist movement has dispelled many of the old stereotypes about women that have prevailed throughout history. We have seen advancements for women in every field imaginable. Presently, we are living in a time where prejudice is not as easily tolerated, allowing for many women to succeed in their chosen profession. Although this is apparent in the corporate world, a lot of improvement still needs to be made in the music business. Although there are more women in music than ever before, stereotypes persist at all levels. The reason for this is the corporate world is more structured and is held more accountable for its practices. On the other hand, the music business does not really belong to any system per se. This allows for many outdated mindsets to remain. Female musicians who are ill-prepared can feel disempowered in this "good old boys" club.

The only way to succeed in a very male-dominated industry is to understand how men work and learn how to work within their structure. Trying to change the "rules of the game" is usually unfruitful and counterproductive. In other words, you have to know the rules and how the game is played if you want to win. The male work environment is set up very much like a game with winners and losers, leaders and followers. The quicker you learn how to maneuver inside this game the more successful you can be. Men feel completely at home in the work environment because they approach their careers with the same mindset as they approach playing a game. For the most part, women don't share this way of thinking so they are at a disadvantage. It's difficult to win a game that you don't know the rules to, or that you don't even know you are playing.

The other mindset that puts women at a disadvantage is the belief that equality means "sameness." Even if women understand there are differences, they may be unaware of how these differences can cause misconceptions. One thing is certain: men think differently about their work than do women, and because the work environment is built around the male structure, men will always have the advantage. Of course, once women understand the rules and how to navigate through the male maze, the field gets leveled. Women are just as capable as men in succeeding in most fields once we are equipped with the necessary tools to succeed. As a female guitarist, you are required to prepare yourself with the right mindset so you will not sabotage yourself along the way.

Following are some of the mistakes that female musicians make when working with men.

MISTAKE NO. 1:
Not Understanding the Importance of Competency

If you've gotten this far with this book, you no doubt understand the need for being competent at what you do. Women can, at times, underestimate the importance of excellence in their careers. The need to appear competent can never be stressed enough when it comes to your skills as a guitarist. You will continually be faced with stereotypical attitudes at all levels, so it is essential when it comes to your abilities that you don't let your guard down. This is easier said than done, particularly if you are just starting out as a guitarist. There may be many areas with which you are presently unfamiliar that can be a dead giveaway to your abilities. Of course, you don't want to try and appear to be something you are not, or try to do something you can't. Your aim should be to do the best at the level you are presently at, to gain as much experience as possible, then move on to the next level. You should always stretch yourself and try to do things that you couldn't before. (On the other hand, you shouldn't put yourself in circumstances beyond what you are capable of handling for the sake of impressing others.) Be as prepared as possible for any opportunity and never reveal your areas of weakness when they come up. Perform in the areas where you feel the most comfortable, but keep your eye on the next opportunity. Always remember, competency is the key that levels the playing field and opens the doors to your success.

MISTAKE NO. 2:
Not Understanding the Importance of Respect

If competency is the key that unlocks the doors to your future, then gaining respect is the field to which the door opens. Gaining respect is of primary importance to a female musician.

For men, obtaining respect is often the number one goal and they will go to great lengths to get it. Also, men respect others who appear competent and professional. They understand how much work it takes to be professional and realize the price someone has to pay to get there. It's not that men don't want to respect you as a musician, they just feel that if you want to play in their game you should know what you are doing and how the game works. You gain respect from your male colleagues when you are viewed as qualified as they are and when you know how to be an integral part of their team. As far as a man is concerned, it is more important to be respected than to be liked, and if you have to choose between the two, you should always choose to be respected.

MISTAKE NO. 3:
Not Being a Team Player

Most boys grew up playing competitive sports and understand the importance of being able to be a team player. They know that to accomplish any goal, the team must work as one unit. They also understand some sacrifices will have to be made and sometimes you have to take a hit for the team. That means that you may have to put aside your personal desires and do something you don't want to do so the team can succeed.

That the majority of women are not really team-friendly is a common complaint of male musicians. Unless you have grown up playing competitive sports, it may be a challenge for you to grasp the need for the team mentality. Competitive sports encourage all the necessary traits that are needed to have a successful team. The team mentality dictates that not only do you sacrifice for the team when needed, but that you keep your personal needs to yourself. Team players are not always loyal to each other and can switch sides if the need arises. However, team players all have the same goal, which is primarily to win their objective. Teams are organized and operate with "one mind."

You may feel that this team thinking doesn't really apply to the music biz, but you would be mistaken. Anywhere men work together, there are these unspoken rules that guide everything they do. The music biz is no exception, and your male musician friends expect you to act like you are part of their team. This is often why women are overlooked for opportunities. We put value on our uniqueness and prefer to be lone rangers believing that our abilities alone are all that is needed to succeed.

MISTAKE NO. 4:
Not Knowing How to Be a Leader

Not only are most women not the ideal team players, many have no clue about how to lead. We often feel that everyone in a group should have their say, and we must be fair at all times. Giving orders does not come across as very feminine and is actually perceived as too aggressive. Since we view our friendships as sacred, we are fearful of offending others and of taking risks in areas that are unknown to us. Men on the other hand are at home with leadership. They have had plenty of opportunities, growing up, to practice their leadership skills. Giving orders is a part of what makes them feel powerful, and they acknowledge that being fair isn't always possible. They aren't afraid of not knowing everything there is to know and are risk-takers when necessary. When they make a mistake, they know how to "spin" it so that it doesn't appear to be so bad. They also know that, for the most part, a team will stick up for a good leader even if he/she occasionally makes mistakes.

To be a successful female in music or any other field, you must not only embrace leadership, but not be afraid of being assertive and decisive. You must also recognize that men will respect your competent leadership even if you make a mistake once in a while.

MISTAKE NO. 5:
Taking Criticism Personally

As women, we are very careful not to say things that would offend others. We take great care in beating around the bush when we do say something that may be perceived as negative. We feel that criticism is harmful to our friendships and avoid it at all costs and are under the impression that it is necessary to be pleasing at all times. This may work well with our female friends but it is not appropriate for a professional musician. Not only are these viewpoints faulty, they stifle our growth. Men understand that criticism is necessary for development and don't take it so personally. They usually recognize that when someone brings a flaw to their attention, it's not because that person doesn't like them. Even if that is the case, they are more apt to put their feelings aside and use negative comments to correct faulty behavior. Of course, men don't always heed advice, but when it comes to their musical career, they are usually eager to make corrections if it means they will advance.

On your journey as a professional guitarist, you should learn to embrace criticism. Many times people will not offer you feedback, so you may not know why you miss opportunities when they arise. Although constructive criticism may be the tool that reveals our blind spots, negative criticism can really hurt. If you have a male mentor you can always ask his opinion about what was said. Either way, learn to deal with criticism, and ask your mentor to offer criticism when he feels you may be doing something that is jeopardizing your success.

Band Tip No. 23—Use Your Full Name
When introducing yourself, use your full name, not your first name or nickname. You're not a waitress. Giving your full name shows that you are professional. In addition, you want people to remember your full name if you get mentioned in a conversation.

MISTAKE NO. 6:
Getting Too Emotional

There is one thing that men dread and that is when women get too emotional or start crying during conflict. Men absolutely dread crying themselves and view it as a sign of weakness. They may even view crying as a tool of manipulation so you can get what you want. Even if you become good buddies with people in your band, crying will still make them uncomfortable.

Let's say you are in a situation in your band where someone has taken out all their anger on you for one reason or another. How do you react? Rather than get emotional and act inappropriately, take time before you respond. Many times women cry because they are trying to hold in what they truly want to say. Be sure to speak up and maintain a professional attitude. If you feel you want to cry you can always take a break and come back later, or you can simply state that you are going to cry and not make a big deal of it. Announcing that you are about to cry may actually stop you from crying and allow you to deal, less emotionally, with issues at hand.

MISTAKE NO. 7:
Putting Up with Inappropriate Behavior

There will surely come a time when you need to address some guy who treats you disrespectfully. We have been taught to be nice to people. Some men view this as a green light to treat women inappropriately. Sometimes, the behavior may consist of sexual advances and other times it may just be downright disrespect. Regardless of the type of behavior it is, you are not expected to tolerate it. Your best approach is always to be as direct as possible and not beat around the bush. If someone has already crossed the line, there is no need to be overly polite. Being too kind can be taken to mean that you are not serious about your request. You can still remain professional, but you may need to be a little pushy. For instance, you may say: "You've crossed the line and you need to back off."

Let's say you are being harassed by some guy who won't back off even after you've warned him. It may be a good idea to let one of your other bandmates know. This can be tricky if they are also buddies. You may have to let the leader be aware of what's going on. If it's a situation where the person who hired you is acting improperly, you may have to remove yourself from the situation completely. As women get older, we tend to put up with less and less bullying, but if you are younger you may feel intimidated about putting someone in their place. Bullies can sense that and use it to their advantage. In any situation where you are being sexually harassed, you should deal with it the best you can before bringing it to anyone else's attention. Unfortunately, even after you tell someone, you may be viewed as the problem, so you will need to tread carefully and use your best judgement. Most importantly, however, never accept harassment as something you must endure in order to succeed.

Band Tip No. 24—Just One of the Boys

Don't confuse bantering with disrespect. When men like you and see you as a team player, they like to tease to show their affection.

MISTAKE NO. 8:
Flirting

Flirting may initially open the doors to opportunities, but it is one of the quickest ways to lose respect. There will always be some form of sexual tension whenever men and women are working together closely, but it is up to you to decide where the line is drawn. Believe it or not, men do not respect overly flirtatious women. That is not to say that they don't like to flirt or don't enjoy the challenge. They will just not treat a women that they are working with respectfully if they consider her to be a flirt, and since respect is the number one thing on your list, you should keep your flirting outside of the working environment.

Another disaster waiting to happen is developing intimate relationships with a guy in the band or someone you are doing business with. Unless you believe this person is your soulmate, it is a very risky endeavor. When the relationship ends, it usually means one of you will have to leave (and believe it or not, it is rarely the man). It's very difficult for women to work with someone with whom they have a past, particularly when it comes to boyfriend/girlfriend relationships.

MISTAKE NO. 9:
Acting Like a Mother or a "Helpless" Girl

By nature, women are a lot more nurturing than men. We are more caring, more available, easier to talk to and basically more concerned about others. Many times, we put other peoples needs before ours, often putting our own needs on hold.

Not only are these motherly qualities not conducive to your career, they can be exhausting. Also, acting like a "helpless" girl puts you in a disempowering position. Projecting the notion that you need to be "taken care of" keeps you at a lower level than the men with whom you are working. It is your responsibility to look after and educate yourself so you know what is going on around you at all times. If you are insecure about things you don't know, then you should be asking your mentor questions and getting advice from him. There is a tendency among younger women to view everyone else as superior. They may have more experience, but you are working with them because they feel you have something to contribute. Therefore, focus on what you are good at and always work on expanding your knowledge so you can feel confident and independent.

Band Tip No. 25—Don't Be Their "Mom"

Never put yourself in the position where you are preparing food for the rest of the band, or picking up when the guys leave a mess behind at a gig. Women often feel like someone needs to take care of the things that the guys miss. That may be so, but it shouldn't be you. By being the one who brings coffee to rehearsals or bakes cookies, you are putting yourself in a position to be treated in a stereotypical fashion. Let the boys bring their own food and pick up after themselves and resist feeling the need to come to everyone's rescue. However, if you are the leader, and a mess is left behind, you should ask them to take care of it, so it does not reflect poorly on you.

MISTAKE NO. 10:
Acting Too Much Like a Man

Just because you are working in a male environment does not mean you need to act like a man. No matter how many years you work around men you will still always be considered a woman. The key is not to try to act like a man, by being tough or trying to carry heavy equipment (unless you can).

There will always be an understanding that you might not be physically as strong as a man, so there is no point trying to prove that you are. The key is to focus on the important issues like leadership and being a team player, and understand how to handle and operate your own gear. Once you have proven you can work with men, they will not respect you any less because you are female.

MISTAKE NO. 11:
Being Too Polite and Humble

Typically, women are a lot more courteous and modest than men. Messages that we have been given from childhood convey that being polite is feminine and that modesty is admirable. In and of themselves, these traits are positive ones, but they can get in the way when it comes to dealing with our competitive male musicians. Men are not afraid to flaunt their skills and aren't considered rude when they make sure they are heard.

Being overly polite and humble can leave us disempowered and feeling insecure when opportunities arise where we need to shine. On the other hand, we don't have to be impolite when we need to get things done. Also, we shouldn't be apologetic about wanting things that are necessary for our careers. It's good to observe your male friends and how they deal with situations versus how you may deal with them. They usually aren't disrespectful, they just don't act overly polite.

MISTAKE NO. 12:
Using Negative Body Language

Many times, we don't notice the impact that our body language has on others around us, particularly men. This is an area that can really sabotage our efforts. People continually send messages to others of how confident they feel and how powerful they see themselves. It is important that we learn how to use our body language to our benefit. For example, women tend to use a lot more expression in their faces. We smile a lot more and nod when others talk to show we are listening. This is appropriate behavior around our friends but does not always work well when dealing with men.

One great way to feel authoritative with your body is to take up a lot of space. If you observe men dealing with conflict, they are totally stone faced. There is no expression on their face. They don't smile to make others feel comfortable. Men tend to be very authoritative and powerful with their bodies. During conflict it is common practice for us to feel uncomfortable and make our body smaller by dropping our shoulders and relaxing our posture. We can gain the appearance of strength by raising our shoulders and standing tall. Practice using gestures that allow you to feel bigger and more authoritative and don't allow others to coerce you. If you are on stage, make sure that you get enough room for yourself to move around. Don't let others cram you in a corner so you have no freedom of movement. If necessary, arrive early at practice or a gig and set up your gear so you have lots of space.

*While still a teenager, **Ani DiFranco** appeared on the New York folk scene of the late 1980s. A prolific writer and recording artist, DiFranco is a leader in the world of independent music. She uses a rhythmic, forceful guitar style, alternate tunings and a rare sense of dynamics to propel her songs about relationships, politics and personal pain and growth. Never one to be boxed in by critics, the business or even the expectations of her own audience, DiFranco continually pushes her own boundaries into new territory.*

Photo by Albert Sanchez

MISTAKE NO. 13:
Using Disempowering Words

Words are just as important as your body language. For example, we tend to always say "sorry" for our mistakes, even unintentional ones. Continually apologizing can make you feel underconfident, which in turn allows others to view you that way as well. Men rarely apologize for their actions and if they make a mistake they will find a way to defend it. For example, men won't bring attention to themselves if they make a mistake in a performance. They will act like it never happened. If they screw up on a booking, instead of claiming responsibility men will find a reason as to why it didn't work out. Listen to yourself during the day and see how many times you use the words "I'm sorry" as a part of your conversation. Try to get out of the habit. Rather than apologizing continually, say something else. For example, if you bump into someone while on stage, rather than saying "I'm sorry," say "Oops, didn't see you there," or something similar. By getting out of the habit of apologizing, you are letting people know that you are not insecure, and that you are confident even when you do make an obvious mistake. Of course, there are times when a formal apology is needed, but save your apologies for such an occasion.

MISTAKE NO. 14:
Treating Everyone as Friends

As women, relationships are very important in our lives. We desire to be connected with others and feel this is an important part of who we are. This is not so for men. Work comes first and relationships second. As a rule, men do not have a need to build great friendships in their workplace. They view colleagues as "work buddies" and keep these relationships in the context of the work environment. They may build friendships that will grow and extend outside of their work, but women tend to have more of a desire for this. Men are also able to work well with people they don't necessarily like. They view the goal of their work as important, and as long as everyone works towards the goal, they will work alongside people they dislike. Women, on the other hand, feel a great need to connect with others and develop friendships where they work. This is not a bad thing but can create problems, especially if some of the relationships don't work out. Women find it difficult to work with people they dislike and have a hard time ignoring conflicts that arise from relationships.

In the music business, it is advisable for women to keep their relationships at a more superficial level than in other environments. This doesn't mean you can't be friendly or have fun, but you need to keep some form of distance between you and your male colleagues. This way, when conflict arises, you can keep your cool and deal with situations in a professional manner. This can seem difficult, particularly in a band setting where people can get close, but there are always lines that should never be crossed if you want to maintain mutual respect.

MISTAKE NO. 15:
Being Catty

Why is it that women enjoy cutting down other women? It's a very bad and immature habit and often reveals insecurities. It's difficult enough for women to make it in the world, they don't need other women causing trouble for them. When men see other men succeed they respect them for their accomplishments. They may feel jealousy and envy, but there is a good chance they will keep these feelings to themselves. Many women, on the other hand, become catty and use slander to put other women down. Usually, when a woman is being catty, it's because she secretly admires this person and feels threatened by her. This is a way of pulling the other person back down to her own level.

When a woman realizes that everyone has their own unique gifts and it is up to each individual to succeed according to her own choices, she will not feel so threatened by someone else's success. Helping other women achieve their goals will only make you more successful. Cutting down another woman is unflattering and juvenile.

MISTAKE NO. 16:
Not Talking Shop or Hanging Out

Men bond differently with other men than women do with other women. Men talk about things they have in common in their work (better known as *talking shop*). Women feel this type of talk is irrelevant and superficial, but for a team of men working together, talking shop is how they pick each other's brains and check out where they really stand in their knowledge. Learning the lingo of your trade is a vital part of being accepted amongst the guys. As a female guitarist, you shouldn't only know about your instrument, you should also learn about music in general. This way, when the guy musicians around you are talking, you can jump in with some interesting fact. Believe it or not, this simple act will gain you much respect and make the guys feel like you fit into their club.

Another significant dynamic to male bonding is hanging out together in a group. This is where friendships are cemented. Even though men don't enjoy talking about intimate things with their buddies, it doesn't mean they don't feel connected with each other. They just build friendships differently than women. Men enjoy doing things together as a team rather than having a one on one chat session with their friends. Once you learn how the dynamics of male friendships work, you will be able to make some lasting relationships with them. If you are looking for more deep, meaningful relationships, you should save that for your girlfriends or your partner.

MISTAKE NO. 17:
Giving Away Too Much Private Information

The less your musician buddies know about you the better. Men aren't really interested in personal stuff anyway. It's always best to keep your conversations along the line of your musical work and goals.

One of the main reasons you shouldn't divulge too much about yourself is because you may be giving off a different perception than you realize. Sometimes, we like to share personal things we are going through and ask for advice. This is the way that we process our experiences and work through them. We get together with our female friends and talk about every intimate detail, asking for our friend's advice on how to proceed. Men, on the other hand, keep personal info to themselves. Since they view problems as weaknesses, they don't like to share what's going on in their lives. By revealing your flaws (even though we all have them) you cause men to evaluate you as a weaker person. Men like to deal with their own situations and keep them to themselves.

MISTAKE NO. 18:
Being Afraid to Use Relationships to Get Ahead

In the music biz, it is definitely true that it's *who* you know that counts. Developing relationships is an integral part of networking. The problem arises when we feel we are "using" other people to get ahead—when we look to them to make connections for us. This is a very female trait. Men understand that the only way to get ahead is to interconnect with others and use their contacts to help them get to the next level.

If you feel you are manipulating someone, you may try a different approach. Let the person know that you are trying to make a connection with so and so and ask them if they would be able to introduce you or if you could use their name as a referral. This way you are giving them the heads up on what you are doing and you won't feel like you are conniving.

Another aspect of this is name-dropping. It is true that people who name-drop too much can be very annoying, but you shouldn't be afraid to mention in a conversation that you have worked with so and so. Letting people know of your connections gives you clout and gives the impression that you have arrived.

MISTAKE NO. 19:
Not Understanding How to Work with Women

While women have no problems taking commands from other men, they resist being told what to do by other women. This is because we have been taught that all women are on the same playing field. No one is above or below you. This mentality can create problems when you are the leader and are working with other women.

Your tactic should be different with women than with men. Men should be treated more standoffish, but women should be treated more like a friend. This way a woman doesn't feel threatened by your position. Because women have been taught from a young age that men have all the authority, they may not be too willing to allow you to wield your authority over them. Around men, you will need to be more assertive and come across confidently. Around women, you will need to develop a friendship and help them understand your position is not to be aggressive but to do your job.

Band Tip No. 26—Watch Your Language

Although swearing for guys is regarded as "cool," you should be careful how far you go with this. Again, it is a respect issue. There is still a double standard that exists, and swearing can bring you down a notch from a male's perspective. If you are looking to be a leader at some point, it's a good practice to avoid swearing.

MISTAKE NO. 20:
Not Understanding the Power of Words

The words you choose, and the way you use them, play an important role in how you are perceived. There are certain things that women do that make them appear weaker, such as not speaking loud enough during a conversation or speaking in a very high-pitched tone. Moreover, speaking too fast or not thinking before one speaks is also a bad habit. There is some form of power that exudes from someone when they pause to think of what they are about to say.

Learning to speak effectively and with poise takes practice. Joining a speaking association like Toastmasters or expanding your vocabulary is a great way to gain confidence and solidify your speaking skills.

CHAPTER 9
TEAM MENTALITY AND LEADERSHIP SKILLS

Often, women are not viewed by men as team players. This shouldn't be surprising, since women and men view teamwork from two completely different perspectives. Women view teamwork as a nucleus of people who all get along, collaborating to meet the needs of all involved. Maintaining individuality allows women to bring their unique gifts to the table. Being fair is of utter importance, as well as keeping within the boundaries of the rules that are set before them. Men, on the other hand, don't need to get along with their team members as long as the other person is getting the job done. They will sacrifice their personal goals to meet the goals of their team. Achieving the goal of the team (winning) is more important than being fair, therefore bending the rules (cheating) is acceptable when necessary.

Another difference between males and females is their approach to leadership. By playing sports, boys at a young age learn to obey the coach, regardless of what he says. They may not always like what they are being told to do, but they know there are consequences in challenging the leader's orders. As boys grow into men, they come to accept that someone is always above or below them in the hierarchy and that the only way to move up any ladder is to do what you've been told. Men who have positions of power will often use loyalty tests to see who does and doesn't respect their authority. A subordinate will understand the need of his leader and respond by doing what he is told, even if the request seems irrational. Since many women have not grown up playing sports or working on teams, they may often object to whoever is in charge if they feel they are being treated unfairly. Because women believe power should be shared, they feel that everyone is equal and has a right to speak their mind. Also, they feel decisions should come through collaboration rather than blindly following orders from one person.

With all these differences in team mentality, it becomes apparent why women struggle in the male environment. As a female guitarist, you will come across many situations where your female perception of teamwork works against you. Your best approach is to learn the rules of those you work with, observing how the male musicians respond to leadership and their attitudes towards the team.

Band Tip No. 27—"Looking Good"

You may have to go the extra mile at times to be perceived as a team player. For instance, you may be expected to be at a gig early to help load in the gear, and yet you will have already spent almost an hour in preparing your hair and face, etc. Most men spend as little as 10 minutes getting ready to go anywhere. This would be something worth mentioning at the next band meeting—that you don't mind helping out, but part of your job is to look good so that needs to be factored into the equation.

BEING A TEAM PLAYER

Webster's New World Dictionary defines a team as "a group of people working or playing together." It also defines a band as "a group of musicians playing together." It appears that band and team are practically synonymous. Therefore, it would make sense that if you are planning to be the guitarist in a band you should understand how to be a team player. Even if you decide to teach guitar instead of performing, or you perform as a solo guitarist, you will still be in an environment where you need to work successfully with other people. The following are some tips that should help you become more familiar with being a team player.

1. **All teams have a goal.** The goal of a band is usually to perform for others just for fun or to make money doing what they love to do. If you are teaching guitar at a music school, the goal of the teachers there will be to educate the students. Music schools have their own rules everyone must abide by, like dress code and following a certain curriculum.

2. **All teams have specific language and topics particular to that team.** Musicians have a certain lingo they use when speaking to each other. Work on becoming familiar with this lingo so you always sound like you know what you are talking about. For instance, most of us are familiar with the word "gig," which means a performance. Other important terms are found in the glossary on pages 37–38. In addition, musicians know all the important players in their own town as well as the names of great famous players. They use these names in conversation to let others know that they are "in the know."

3. **Team members are not necessarily loyal to one another.** Even if you become friends with all the members of your band, this doesn't mean they will remain with you for their whole career. When better opportunities arise, they may decide to leave your band for greener pastures. Women have greater difficulty leaving a band since they tend to view their bandmates as friends, but men, who view their friendships as secondary, will have less of a problem departing.

4. **Teams sacrifice their individuality for the goal.** Because a team is a nucleus of people aiming for the same purpose, there are times when you will need to forfeit your individuality. For instance, your band may want to start doing more corporate events where you are performing to a mainstream audience. In a situation like this, you may not be able to play the type of music that you would normally play, or you may have to dress more conservatively than you would if you were in a bar.

5. **Members of a team may not all like each other.** Bands tend to be famous for conflict, which many times can tear a band apart. It's important to realize that you don't need to like everyone to work with them. In most teams, like in sports, players just accept the fact that some of their teammates rub them the wrong way. They understand that every member is important and sometimes the most obnoxious players are the best on their team. This is a little trickier in a band situation where members work very closely together. Because women feel hypocritical working with people they dislike, they find this aspect of being a team player difficult. The best approach is to always maintain a professional attitude and rise above your feelings about another person.

6. **Members of a team understand the importance of meetings.** Bonding between band members doesn't only occur while they are performing together. Male musicians who perform for a living view their gigs as a time to hang with their buddies. This is a time when they might share a drink or talk shop. This type of behavior may seem unimportant to women, but it is during these times that men get to know each other better and build trust. This bond will come in handy in the future if band members move on to other bands. If you've built a "buddy" relationship with them, they will feel more inclined to recommend you to other musicians or people who are in a position of power. So, rather than taking off during your breaks when you are at a gig, use this opportunity to "hang" with the guys. Or, if after a band rehearsal everyone wants to go out, make the effort and go with them. You will be building lasting relationships for the future and be treated as a true team player.

7. **Team players know there is only one leader.** When a group of men work together, they understand that whatever the leader says is to be obeyed. Even if men don't necessarily agree with the leader, they recognize that for a team to be successful, only one person can lead and others must follow. At times, this can seem difficult to women, who are used to collaborating with others to arrive at a common solution that seems fair for all involved. Unfortunately, when a women objects to what her leader is asking of her, she is not viewed as a team player. Even if her objections are valid, the leader will feel like he is being challenged. Men are not familiar with collaboration and expect that a team player follows their leader. This is where a lot of women fall into problems in bands. They feel that they should be able to be a part of the solution and talk through any difficulties. This may work well for a band that has been together for a long time where everyone is familiar with the other players, but for the most part, if you are being hired to do a specific job, you will be expected to do what is asked of you. If you don't agree, you can always talk to the leader after a gig or rehearsal and bring forth your objections, but if the leader is not willing to compromise, your best bet is to follow his/her wishes.

LEADERSHIP SKILLS

Leadership is the ability to influence those around you. Good leaders aren't afraid to take risks or initiate ideas. They are able to anticipate and solve problems. They are effective and organized planners and focus on priorities. Leaders also understand that people are very important and that building relationships is not a waste of time. Very few people are born leaders. Most people have to develop certain skills before becoming successful at leadership.

Unfortunately, women rarely grow up in an environment where they are given the opportunity to lead. At a young age, girls regard leadership with disdain, since telling others what to do is not conducive to developing good relationships. If they happen to be natural leaders, they are viewed as pushy and too aggressive. Girls tend to thrive in a flat environment where decisions are negotiated upon and no one has the upper hand over anyone else. One of the greatest disadvantages is that those women who actually are in a leadership position rarely mentor younger women. Therefore, a woman who is desirous of becoming a leader has little information at her disposal.

Boys at a young age are encouraged to take on leadership roles. Usually these opportunities arise in the games they play. Giving orders is a demonstration of their power and masculinity. Other boys have no problem taking orders from their peers since they know that at some point they will be in the same position. Even though boys may not know everything about leading, they are more willing to take chances, even if it means falling on their face. If they are unsure of certain things, they pretend to know what they are doing. Boys usually have many mentors who support their leadership efforts, from their peers to their teachers as well as their parents.

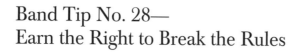

Band Tip No. 28—
Earn the Right to Break the Rules
Once you have gained respect and are regarded as a leader or a team player, you can introduce some of your femininity to situations when appropriate. The trick is learn the rules, then break them.

Band Tip No. 29—Assertive Leadership

Being an assertive leader in a male dominated band takes practice. It can feel unnatural to give other people orders. One thing to focus on is that men expect their leaders to be assertive, decisive and give commands. If you are the leader, they are waiting for you to act as a leader and will listen to you if you show that you are confident with your position.

HOW TO BE AN EFFECTIVE LEADER

Leadership opportunities will arise frequently in your musical career. To make things happen, you will need to step up to the plate. Although being a leader can be daunting, you can learn by observing successful leaders around you. There are also many books written that can teach you proficiency in leadership, such as *Developing the Leader Within You* by John C. Maxwell. Perhaps your most common opportunities will occur while you are in a band setting, but this may not always be the case. Actually, when you are teaching someone how to play guitar, you are in fact acting in a leadership role. Or, down the road you may decide to open up a music school of your own where you will be the person in charge of hiring and firing teachers. Whatever arises, take every opportunity you can to practice being a leader. By taking small steps now, you will find that your expertise and confidence will increase.

Following are some tips for being a good leader in music or in any situation.

1. **Your approach to leadership will reflect your personality.** Your personality often reflects the type of leader you will be. If you are very outgoing and direct, chances are your leadership will mirror these qualities. If you are more introverted and non-confrontational, your leadership style will take on those qualities. For instance, if you are the leader of your band and you're very gregarious by nature, you will probably deal with other band members more directly and be more expressive with your viewpoints.

2. **Different situations call for different leadership styles.** There are times when you will need to be very assertive when you are leading. A good example is if you are performing with a lot of inexperienced players. Since they will be unsure of how everything is done, they will be looking to you to give them most of the instructions. In a situation like this, you need to be more direct and feel comfortable giving orders. You don't need to be over-assertive, but come across confidently, like you know what you are talking about. On the other hand, when you are dealing with band members that are more experienced, you can take more of a supportive role, more like what a coach does.

3. **Leading men is different than leading women.** When you are the leader of a group of men, they will expect you to be decisive. They regard their leader as a person with power who is able to make decisions when necessary. They expect to be led and get frustrated when women are indecisive. Your best approach when leading a group of male musicians is to assert your authority and stick to your decisions. When you are leading a group of women, you will receive better results if you work alongside them in the decision making process. Women have not been accustomed to being told what to do by other women in power, therefore being too assertive may backfire. On the other hand, you will need to demonstrate to your female colleagues that you are the one in charge. You can ask for opinions, but any final decision should be yours. It can be quite challenging leading women, and you may find that your relationships can get shaken. The bottom line is that you must accept the fact that not all women will celebrate your position.

4. **Leaders don't back down during difficult times.** As a leader, you will experience challenging situations that might make you feel like backing down; your body language may even make you appear smaller. However, you should never back away from the power that has been given to you to lead. Stand tall and face challenges head on. The men around you will see how you are dealing with situations and respect you for it.

5. **Leaders are great problem solvers.** If you can prove you are effective at solving problems, you will be regarded as a good leader by those around you. You should try to be prepared before problems occur. For instance, you may be performing with your band at an outdoor event. The weatherman has predicted there might be rain. You decide to bring some plastic coverings to protect the gear in case the forecast becomes a reality. You may also inquire of the event planner what alternate plans are in place in case of rain. Be sure to let your band know that you have already pre-planned for the rain. This demonstrates your ability to plan for a variety of scenarios.

6. **Good leaders have great attitudes.** Have you ever noticed that wherever there is a group of people working together, the overall characteristic of that group is determined by the leader? For instance, some corporations have very authoritarian leaders, causing everyone under them to be uptight and fearful. The same is true in any form of leadership. Attitudes are filtered down from the top all the way to the bottom of a group of people. As a leader in the music business, your attitude affects those around you. If you want to have a positive band, you, as the leader, must set the precedent. Even when you are having a bad day, you should still rise above your feelings and project your ability to handle difficulties in a constructive manner.

7. **Good leaders have integrity.** One of the quickest ways to gain respect as a leader is to do what you say you will do. Nothing is more disappointing to those around you than making promises that never come to fruition. People around you will test your position as a leader. Doing what you say is a good way to prove that your decisions have weight. If you don't think you can come through with something don't mention it in the first place, or simply say you are trying to make such and such happen and will keep them informed of the progress.

8. **Great leaders know how to deal with interpersonal conflicts.** One of the greatest difficulties is dealing with conflict that arises in your band. Since women tend to get more emotional than men when dealing with conflict, you will need to learn how to keep a cool attitude during disagreements. A common problem may arise when a man you are working with challenges your authority. Men tend to test the boundaries of people above them to see where they stand in the hierarchy. You must be prepared to stand your ground and not back away from your position of power. At times like these, you may need to be very assertive. You should never feel you need to apologize for decisions you make, even if they weren't the best. Using anger as a way of demonstrating power can be an effective tool in conflict, but only if it is not your normal behavior. Anger can be your ace in the hole that you can pull out to show you mean business. But keep in mind that you must remain professional and not emotional when you get angry. Having a "stone face" and a confident stance is helpful in letting others know that you will not be wavering in your point of view.

Band Tip No. 30—Carry a Business Card

Always carry your business card. You never know when you will meet other musicians who may want to hire you or an agent who wants to book you into one of his rooms. Your business card should always be up-to-date with your present phone number and website. Don't scratch out old numbers or write new info on the card. Although it costs more to redo cards, it will make you money in the long run because people will view you as a pro.

*A soulful vocalist, **Bonnie Raitt** is also one of the few women known for bottleneck-slide playing. Since 1971, her unique fusion of blues, rock and R&B has brought her consistent critical acclaim. However, it wasn't until the release of her Grammy-award winning album* Nick of Time *in 1989 that she began to enjoy real commercial success.*

CHAPTER 10
FINDING A MENTOR AND
FINDING YOUR OWN NICHE

Band Tip No. 31—Finding a Mentor

If you are not sure where to start looking for a mentor, think of all the people with whom you are familiar who have music experience. Perhaps a music teacher at school also performs on the weekends around your city. Don't be afraid to approach people and see if you could ask them a few questions about the music business. You'd be surprised at how willing people are to help.

MENTORS

Mentors are people who are willing to teach you the ropes in a particular field. If you want to succeed as a guitarist, one of the quickest ways is to find a mentor. In any business, research has shown that having a mentor is probably the most important factor in attaining your goals.

In the search for a mentor, keep in mind there are different types of mentors. For instance, a guitar teacher is a mentor. He/she is the person who has already spent all the time necessary to become proficient at playing guitar. The reason you study with a music teacher is because you recognize that they know something you don't, and that they are able to help you reach your goals quicker than on your own.

You will need several mentors on your musical journey. Let's say you have a great guitar teacher and have learned a lot from your lessons, but you know nothing about the music business. Rather than trying to figure out everything yourself, you will want to seek out a mentor. You may not feel it is necessary to have someone teach you about the business, but the fact that you are reading this book and learning new things shows how important it is to learn from others. Why would you want to spend years learning something on your own, making mistakes and getting frustrated, when you can pick up a book and read in several hours what it took the author 20 years to learn?

Books are an excellent source of mentorship and can cut your learning curve tremendously. Learning from an experienced person is a very powerful tool. Also, having a male mentor who can help you understand important aspects of working with men will be very insightful. There are many things you will need to learn in this male-dominated business, and a male mentor can help you on your path tremendously. Also, having someone knowledgeable to talk to during trying times can put you at ease. This doesn't mean you should not have a female mentor, particularly if you can find a woman who is a little older and has lots of experience. This may be a little trickier though, since there aren't as many around.

So, what can a mentor actually do for you? People who have been around for a while have a lot of street knowledge you can't get from books. Sometimes, that includes knowing what *not* to do or say in certain situations. As well, a mentor who is local to your area can warn you against certain people you may want to avoid. This includes those who would take advantage of young inexperienced players hungry for opportunities. These people can be very convincing and manipulative and end up wasting a lot of your time. Mentors can also guide you in the development of your skills as well as offer advice on practical goal-setting. They can direct you on the right path in general, identifying blind spots along the way and showing you how to correct them.

We all have areas that need improvement and sometimes we aren't necessarily sure how to fix them. If you build a good relationship with a mentor, he/she will feel more comfortable in being honest with you. Never take criticism personally, since it is the only way to improve. You may not agree with everything your mentor says about you or your playing, but criticism usually has some truth to it.

The key is to have plenty of mentors. You may have one main person who is willing to help you, but that shouldn't stop you from getting advice from as many people as possible, especially at the start of your career. There will come a time when you won't need to be asking so many questions or where it is inappropriate to ask questions; for example, if you are leading a band and need to appear informed, confident and decisive.

Band Tip No. 32—Networking

If you have a mentor who really believes in you and your talent, they may help you connect with powerful people or deal with situations in your band. As mentioned earlier, networking is vitally important in the music business and your opportunities would be very limited without it. People who have been in the business for a long time may know all the key players and even have some influence with them. They may know people in radio, or TV or may have access to producers and record people. Even if they don't know these people, they may introduce you to people who do. As well, there is a feeling of giving back by helping someone who is just starting out in their career.

FINDING YOUR OWN NICHE

Have you ever heard a recording of a guitarist or vocalist and were able to immediately identify who it was? Maybe it was their style of music that seemed familiar, or the particular sound of their guitar. The reason you could recognize the artist was because he or she had their own unique sound.

When you have been playing guitar for a while, you will start to feel drawn to certain styles or sounds of music. For instance, you may really like the sound of a particular type of guitar or amp or maybe a combination of certain guitar effects. Whatever it is, something will resonate with you and you will get a sense that this is what you really enjoy playing. You may feel that you lean more towards a heavier type of music, or you may really enjoy the picking techniques of an acoustic. This is a natural development of your own signature style and something that you should aim to cultivate. All great musicians can be identified by a distinctive quality in their playing or sound, and this should be your eventual intent as well.

Band Tip No. 33—Being Original

Developing your own sound if you are in an original band is very important if you want to get signed with a record label. You need to stand out from the crowd and offer something with a little twist. There are plenty of bands that copy other bands, but originality is what record companies are looking for. Remember, though, that record companies are all about selling CDs, so you must also fit into the commercial format.

One way to identify your natural niche is through writing your own music. Even if you are not inclined to sing, that doesn't mean you can't write instrumental guitar music. You will find that by creating your own arrangements, you will be able to come up with a style that is unique. Although at this point in time, almost every type of music under the sun has been performed by some artist or other, that doesn't mean that you can't develop something a little different. We all are influenced by someone else, but we can take their style to the next level or add something to it that makes it different. All great guitarists admit to being influenced by someone else, but when you listen to them you can tell that they have their own way of playing. That is why it's so important for you to listen to a lot of great players from every type of music. The more open-minded you are, the more you will be able to draw on different sources of music and put your own spin on it. Rarely can you find someone who just comes up with a completely new style never heard before. Usually, new styles are combinations of other styles that developed through time and came out sounding new and fresh.

Another way to determine what works for you is to listen to feedback from people around you. Sometimes when you are performing or jamming with others, someone will make a comment to you that they really liked the way you interpreted a certain passage of music. They may hear something in your style that you are unable to pinpoint just yet. Take note of what they say and try and develop it on your own time and see what comes out of it. It may be your own style beginning to surface. Developing your own niche takes time, but if you make an effort and allow yourself to experiment with various sounds and techniques, something original will emerge.

GIVING BACK

After all is said and done, there comes a time in your career that you will feel you want to contribute to others. Once your career is well on its way, it's a good time to help those around you who are trying to find their way as well. Helping others by being a mentor, by teaching, or by doing clinics can be very rewarding. Even if teaching isn't your forte, being able to offer advice to a novice musician can make you feel that you are building the music business and passing the torch to the next generation.

There will always be young, up-and-coming musicians who will admire what you do and dream of one day being able to play like you. By taking the time to help them find their way, you will feel like you have come full circle. Particularly, by teaching younger, inexperienced women the ropes of the business and the complexities of working with men, you will be making it easier for them—in turn, making it easier for the next generation.

Photograph by Tad Hershorn, June 1989, Houston

Emily Remler (1957–1990) *was one of the few female guitarists to earn the respect of the jazz community. Her untimely death at the age of 32 was a shock to the jazz world. She attended Berklee in 1976 and recorded a duo album,* Together, *with Larry Coryell in 1985.*

CHAPTER 11
INTERVIEWS

This last chapter features interviews with three prominent female guitarists in the music business. **Lisa Loeb**, whose career spans from radio hit phenomenon to flourishing actress, talks about the importance of music education, as well as networking in order to further one's career. **Alexx Calise**, who has a very promising career as a guitarist/singer/songwriter, offers her take on the importance of practicing and being competent. **Allison Robertson** (from the Donnas), with her raw rock-prowess, gives us a behind-the-scenes glimpse into being successful in an all-girl band. These three perspectives offer valuable insight into the process of becoming a successful female musician.

LISA LOEB

Lisa Loeb grew up in Dallas, Texas. She played piano as a young girl but eventually switched to the guitar. Lisa studied music theory and piano and wrote her first original songs in her teens. She received a degree in comparative literature from Brown University and later attended Berklee School of Music in Boston. She has had her own cooking show *Dweezil and Lisa,* and has also starred on the *Drew Carey Show* and *House on Haunted Hill.* Presently, Lisa is hosting the reality show *#1 Single,* which is aired on Entertainment Television. Even though she has a wide variety of talents, music still remains one of her passions.

Photo courtesy of Daisy Rock Guitars

Vivian Clement (VC): You perform mostly with a guitar although you originally started out playing the piano. Why did you decide to become a guitarist?

Lisa Loeb (LL): There are many reasons I switched to guitar. My main reason was that I realized pretty much the only time I played or practiced piano was when I was sitting next to my piano teacher during a lesson. My family valued the arts, and I couldn't just stop playing piano without learning how to play another instrument, so I discussed it with my father. We decided that guitar would be the right change: I'd continue with lessons to learn more about music theory, classical music and jazz, [but] I'd learn how to play popular songs [on the guitar] and I'd also have something that I could play quietly in my room. I started with an acoustic guitar, but soon purchased a Fender Strat with a Peavey Backstage amp too. I had started writing when I was about six years old, but with the guitar I began to write more songs with lyrics. I continue to play piano, but guitar is my primary instrument. It's easier to carry around too! At the time, I had friends at summer camp who brought their guitars with them, I loved so many rock bands, especially the Police, and I looked up to the boys who played music in assemblies in high school. I wanted to do what they were doing.

VC: For the most part, you perform with an acoustic guitar. Do you find it has advantages over an electric?

LL: The acoustic guitar is a lighter instrument. Seriously, it's easier on the body to carry around. I used to play electric much more, but it got a little crazy carrying it around in the electric guitar cases and then the amp, well, that's another story! I didn't have casters on my amp growing up, so I used to lug the amp and the guitar around. I love playing electric guitar, but it's easier to play acoustic when I travel.

VC: *What recommendations do you have for female singer/songwriters who want to improve their guitar playing?*

LL: I suggest getting a great teacher, learning all the classic theory, including reading, ear training, studying all kinds of guitar playing styles: classical, Spanish, rock, folk, finger picking and more. Practice a lot. Play with a metronome. Have no fear. I think that fear and embarrassment get in the way of a great guitar solo. Remember that you have to start somewhere. Oh yes, also make sure to have your guitar set up properly: the guitar will "feel" better and is much more fun to play.

VC: *There are many young female guitarists popping up in the music scene today, what is your advice to those who want to play guitar professionally?*

LL: Make sure you can read, communicate musically, know many styles, know your gear and all of the other skill-related things. To be a professional, you must make contacts in the music world. Meet people in bands who are looking for guitar players for live gigs and studio gigs. Make business cards—be easy to get a hold of. Do free sessions if that's what it takes to prove yourself in the studio. Get yourself out there and act professionally. Let other guitar players know that you're looking for gigs. Sometimes people have conflicts and need someone to fill in for them.

VC: *You are affiliated with Daisy Rock Guitars as well as Fender Hello Kitty (fenderhellokitty.com). What is the reason for associating yourself with these "very female" organizations?*

LL: I love the way Daisy Rock Guitars look and I've always loved Hello Kitty, so that was a natural match. I think it's fun to work with companies who encourage people to play guitar. I've also worked with Taylor guitars, Gibson and Peavey in the past.

VC: *You studied at Berklee School of Music. How has music education influenced your musicianship and your career?*

LL: I only attended Berklee for a summer program a few years after I graduated from Brown University. However, I studied music my entire life. Music education has taught me how to communicate with other musicians. It's given me the knowledge to feel comfortable in recording studios, and it's given me the tools to continue learning along the way. Music education teaches specific skills, but it also teaches how to keep your ears open, how to meet other musicians and form a continually growing community, and also how to have disciplined practice habits. Music education gives you the ability to learn as well as to continue to ask questions without being embarrassed!

VC: *It appears that you are quite knowledgeable when it comes to drums. How has this knowledge shaped the outcome of your songs while writing and performing?*

LL: I'm not a great drummer at all! I love drums and work with drummers all the time. The more I know about the different instruments and what I expect from players, the easier it is to communicate with the other folks with whom I'm playing. Sometimes I have definite drum sounds and parts in my head when I'm writing, and other times I really collaborate with the drummers.

VC: *The music industry is still very male-dominated. Have you seen attitudes change towards women since you started your career?*

LL: I feel like the music industry hasn't changed very much. Although there are some really strong, talented women musicians including Bonnie Raitt, Sheryl Crow, Joni Mitchell and many others, it's still male-dominated. I still hear, "You play really well," and I know that the part they're not saying is, "for a girl." Seriously.

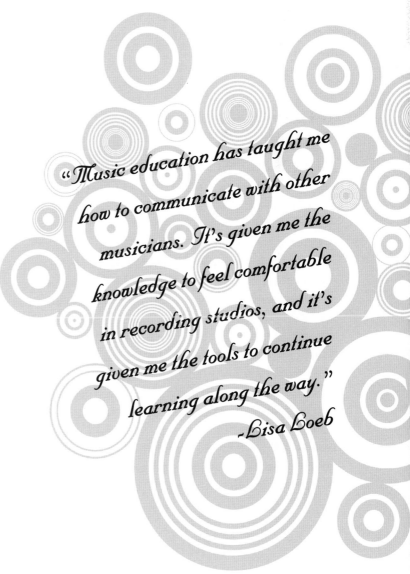

"Music education has taught me how to communicate with other musicians. It's given me the knowledge to feel comfortable in recording studios, and it's given me the tools to continue learning along the way."
–Lisa Loeb

VC: *What advice would you give female musicians when they are dealing primarily with men in the business?*

LL: Just be yourself and don't get wimpy. At the same time, don't feel like you have to be masculine if you're going to deal with a lot of men. You can still be a girl/gal/woman. Be straightforward. In some cases, you might have to make sure you have some strong men on your team (attorneys, managers, other musicians) in order to be taken seriously. I know it's really lame, but it's true.

VC: *Some of your accomplishments include your own cooking show* Dweezil and Lisa. *You've also starred on the* Drew Carey Show *as well as the* Chris Isaac Show, *and the film* House on Haunted Hill. *Recently you starred in* #1 Single, *a reality show centering around your life as a single woman. How have all of these endeavors helped your music career?*

LL: Music is my primary career, but I enjoy acting and telling stories in other ways as well. Lucky for me, there is a lot of acceptance when musicians do all of the things they enjoy. By being able to work in different fields, I'm able to keep music fresh for myself. It's all an extension of my being a human being and communicating with others.

ALEXX CALISE

Alexx Calise is a bold, young singer, songwriter and guitarist. Inspired by her musical idols, she began playing guitar at age 11. She quickly developed her own lyrical style and impressive guitar chops. Her debut CD, *Morning Pill,* was released in 2007, and she is currently gearing up for her first national tour.

Photograph by Jon Scott Photos, courtesy of Alexx Calise

VC: *You started playing guitar at age 11. What made you decide to play guitar?*

Alexx Calise (AC): My father inspired me to pick up the guitar when I was 11. As kids, my brother and I would sit on the floor while my dad played us the James Bond theme song and "Michelle" from the Beatles. It was hypnotic for me and I would just sit there, mesmerized, somehow knowing that one day I would master this instrument. As soon as I held a guitar in my hands, I fell in love. I began playing rhythm and blues, rock and grunge, locking myself away in my room every day for hours. Of course, I had to start with learning my then-current rock idol's power chords, which led to distortion, loud amps and angry neighbors. I spent all of my allowance and babysitting money on new guitars and gear, instead of Barbie dolls and makeup, which all my friends were interested in. As a child I was pretty reserved, but whenever I got a hold of a guitar, I'd just get crazy and just have to rock out. For me, it was, and is, a primal instinct.

VC: *Who are some of your main influences?*

AC: As I progressed in my learning, I was influenced by many different musicians from many different genres. Some of the artists that really resonated with me were Stone Temple Pilots and Silverchair for their crunchy distortion; the Toadies for their use of odd time signatures; Buckcherry and Aerosmith for their attitude; Our Lady Peace, the Doors and Jeff Buckley for their clever lyrics and wordplay; and Kenny Wayne Shepherd and Stevie Ray Vaughan for their soulful, ripping guitar riffs.

VC: *Although you started out being self-taught, have you had any formal musical training?*

AC: While most of my guitar skills were self-taught, I did have some formal training. Patience is a virtue that I still struggle with, but I possessed even less of it as a child. So, as my hunger for music knowledge increased, I wasn't content with just figuring things out for myself; I had to be able to perform complex solos immediately. Luckily, my instructor was a bit unorthodox and he agreed to teach me what I wanted to learn first before actually showing me the typical scales and theory. When I first came to him, I was this little 13 year-old, flannel-wearing grunge girl that played Silverchair and Korn songs. Now that I think of it, the first song I ever learned on guitar was Silverchair's "Tomorrow." I remember agonizing over the solo at the end, but when I finally got it, the sense of accomplishment I felt was unparalleled. It was amazing to me, I could actually perform a pentatonic scale!

Listening to the blues was another textbook for me and I learned a lot from Kenny Wayne Shepherd and Stevie Ray Vaughan. Sitting by myself, I would try mimicking their incredibly complex solos, which led to me accidentally creating many intricate guitar solos of my own.

"I do love the fact that I inspire young girls to pick up the guitar, as I think they're often intimidated because it's generally only played by males. I want to show that girls can rock as hard or, dare I say, harder than the boys!"
~ Alexx Calise

VC: *What type of gear do you own?*

AC: I am a total gear head. I currently have 23 guitars, three different guitar amp rigs, a multitude of microphones, outboard effects, pedals, boards and wireless gear. My favorites are my Daisy Rock Dark Star Custom, my Fender Stratocaster (first guitar I ever owned), my Hughes and Kettner Triamp rig, most of my Rocktron pedals and my Sennheiser mics and in-ear monitor system.

VC: *What is your practicing routine like?*

AC: A typical practice session for me is pretty rigorous. I usually run through my scales and my existing songs, and then when I'm done, I songwrite. That's my big "treat." Although, I don't consider doing what I love to do "work" or "practice." I don't really think about it; I just do it. However, I try to switch things up a bit, and even combine elements. Sometimes I'll rehearse both voice and guitar in one shot by running up and down the scales on both instruments for a few hours. There isn't any right or wrong way to do it, I just make sure that no matter how tired I am or how little sleep I got the night before, I make it a priority.

VC: *What are some of your goals as a female guitarist?*

AC: My ultimate goal as a female guitarist is to play so well that nobody can tell I'm a girl just by listening to me. You see, I'm always being told that I play guitar like a guy; and while I know it's meant as a compliment, it's insulting to think that a female is somehow genetically inferior. I don't want to be an outstanding "female" guitar player; I want to be an outstanding guitar player. Like Stevie Ray Vaughan was or Eddie Van Halen. As dedicated as I am, I have to be realistic, so I set small goals for myself. If I'm having trouble with certain rhythmic patterns or I'm learning new chords for a song, I play until I get it right.

I do love the fact that I inspire young girls to pick up the guitar, as I think they're often intimidated because it's generally only played by males. I want to show that girls can rock as hard or, dare I say, harder than the boys!

VC: *You also enjoy songwriting. How do you incorporate your guitar playing into your songwriting?*

AC: When it comes to songwriting, I usually write chord progressions and music to my already written lyrics. The mood and content of my lyrics generally dictate what the music will sound like. Usually my songs allow me to employ the inverted chords and distortion that I love because I tend not to write sugary, insipidly sweet, pop songs.

VC: *What challenges have you encountered trying to incorporate your playing, songwriting and singing?*

AC: Combining songwriting, playing and singing into a busy life can be quite intimidating. Luckily for me, I usually don't have a problem because I write quickly and with very little effort. My songs are usually channeled from somewhere, and just seem to come to me when I put myself into the right frame of mind. Inside my head is a very busy place and I have songs coming and going all day long. It's just a matter of finding a moment of peace and quiet, comfort, pulling the songs out and putting all the pieces together.

VC: *How have you worked on developing your voice?*

AC: Voice development for me is pretty simple: I just sing! Everywhere—in the car, in the shower, wherever I can. Besides the occasional vocal lesson for maintenance, I'm self taught. The things I try to focus on most for myself are volume and range. I'm a very soft-spoken singer at times, so I try little things to bring my voice out. Usually, I just experiment. I get angry, I scream, I try to bring it all out from the depths. I also try not to get comfortable with a specific range. I like to challenge myself and sing higher or lower than normal, regardless of what it sounds like. I practice it until it's flawless. If I can do something without screwing up at least 14 or 15 times in a row, then I know I've got it.

VC: *What have you found has changed since you have become a professional working musician?*

AC: Since I became a full-time working musician, a lot has changed. The most important thing is that I actually get *paid*. It's a beautiful thing. All kidding aside, I've changed as a person. You find out who you really are and who your true friends are. There's a lot more work involved as well—watching what I eat, staying fit, photo and video shoots, keeping my chops up, doing interviews, answering emails, etc. It's two full-time jobs. I find I have less and less free time, but it's okay because I'm doing what I love. It is truly a blessing to be doing what I've always wanted to do with my life.

VC: *What advice can you offer to girls/women who want to make playing guitar a career?*

AC: The best advice I can offer anyone reading this who wants a career as a guitarist is start immediately! And especially for women; there's really a dearth of female rockers these days...we need more of them. Express yourself, and be yourself. Don't ever let anyone tell you that because you're a girl, you can't rock out with the best of them. There is an unlimited amount of success out there in the universe that is yours for the taking, so get out there and lay claim to your share.

ALLISON ROBERTSON

In 1993, Allison Robertson and three of her best friends started a band and began rehearsing after school. After several name changes, they settled on the Donnas, and Robertson adopted the stage name Donna R. The Donnas began recording and touring the world while still in high school. Their commercial breakthrough came with the 2002 album *Spend the Night.* Still together with their original lineup, the Donnas have refined their sound through the years to become one of the tightest rock bands around.

Photo by Alison Krick

VC: *What is the difference between playing with an all-girl band and a band with guys?*

Allison Robertson (AR): The biggest difference in playing with an all-girl band as opposed to a guy band is that you are putting yourself in the minority automatically, merely by existing. There are far fewer females in bands than males, especially in the rock world, so no matter what the music, look or attitude of the band happen to be, you will be placed in the category of "female bands" and considered a rare breed by many who have never seen one before.

VC: *Do you think that being in an all-girl band could give you an advantage in the music business?*

AR: The irony to being singled out as a freakish sideshow "girl band" in a sea of males is that you *are* different, and it generates interest based on that point alone. People flock to see girls play in bands just because they've never seen it before. The problem is that they sometimes have lower expectations of female players, which is obviously upsetting but nevertheless apparent. I feel that female bands should consciously work on their skill and really hone their chops before playing live for this reason, because every doubting heckler needs to be put in their place and realize that men and women are equal when it comes to playing music.

VC: *You commented before that you're not competitive. What suggestions would you offer to girls who still need to prove they are competent guitarists?*

AR: I think girls that play guitar need to be competitive only with themselves. As long as you keep pushing yourself, you will get better every time, and that's something that shows in your performance. There will always be someone who plays faster, who looks cooler, who has better equipment, but in the end you only can be responsible for yourself. You need to take pride in your achievements and constantly take your skills to the next level!

VC: *What advice would you give a female guitarist who wants to start her own all-girl band?*

AR: I believe it's necessary to find other girls to play with who are compatible as friends as well as musicians. Sure, you want to find a great drummer, etc., but you need to be able to trust these girls, to feel like family with them, because girl bands can't last out there unless they are a tight, proud unit. Think of your band as a gang of aliens who mean well and are great musicians, but everyone you encounter just laughs and provokes you because you have big alien heads and no one even notices the music. Your girls can help you shut out the negatives and maintain a strong center of gravity.

VC: *How have you dealt with stereotypical attitudes towards yourself as a female guitarist?*

AR: Well, one thing most female musicians have to deal with is the comments: "You play great for a girl!" or, "I've never seen a girl play like that before!" These are *not* compliments, yet usually the person who says these things thinks they are giving you a huge compliment! The other problem I run into a lot is that people seem to think girls are weaker and can only handle "girly guitars" (lighter, smaller, etc.). Some people are just impressed that a girl like me can play a Les Paul. It's not that heavy, dude! It's not impressive—it's absolutely normal. One last thing that is hard to deal with as a female guitarist is the comparisons to others. I don't feel intimidated or compelled to compete with other female guitarists, but fans and concert-goers do feel the need to say things like, "So-and-so is a lot faster than you," or "Do you think so-and-so is copying you? She has the same guitar." These kinds of things are meant to get a catty reaction out of us girls, but it's important be supportive of your sister bands, not jealous.

VC: *What has been the most difficult thing to overcome in the music business?*

AR: The most difficult thing to overcome in the music business is the whole obsession with image over talent. Being female means (to most of the music industry) that no matter what you sound like, you can be poked and prodded into being sexier, cuter and girlier, which equals money for them. The more you fight to stay true to your own style, visually and musically, the more you get pinned as "difficult" or "bratty." There is enough room for female pop stars, dancers and rock bands to co-exist in harmony, but the unfortunate reality is that you're all competing against each other for the same "female" slot on radio, TV, etc.

VC: *Most of your tunes are rock-based. Do you experiment with other genres?*

AR: I really like classical music. I used to play violin for a little while when I was a kid, but I gave up because I was pretending to read music and realized I'd have to actually learn it if I wanted to keep advancing! The competition was stiff back then in elementary school. I also like country, especially female songwriters and players. I'm a huge Emmylou Harris fan. I'm not currently working on any other projects right now, but I believe in keeping my ears open to new sounds all the time, because you never know what ideas you'll get from listening outside of the box.

VC: *What gear do you presently own?*

AR: I own a lot of Gibson guitars, some from the factory and some that I've collected on tours, trolling through different vintage guitar stores. I have a few Les Paul Standards, a '79 Custom, two Studios, two SG Classics, a Melody Maker, a TV Yellow Junior, an L6-S, a Les Paul Recording, lots of interesting, odd guitars that don't sound like any others. My favorite is called the "Spirit," which is like a double-cutaway Jr. with humbuckers. It's rare and strange and beautiful. I also play through Marshalls and currently use the JCM 2000s but have my eye on some other pieces. Onstage I often use a Fender Vibrolux amp as well to add definition to my tone. For pedals, I usually use just a Boss equalizer to boost my mids for soloing and sometimes a Boss chorus as well; I like pedals but I've never liked feeling like I have to "hang out" by the pedal board—I prefer to run around the stage completely uninhibited.

"Well, one thing most female musicians have to deal with is the comments: 'You play great for a girl!' or, 'I've never seen a girl play like that before!' These are not compliments, yet usually the person who says these things thinks they are giving you a huge compliment!"
– Allison Robertson

VC: How do you incorporate business skills with musical skills?

AR: I've never been the most business-minded in my group, but I think it's important to acknowledge the business end of things when I write and when I play onstage, because I think of this as my job, not just my hobby, and I want to reach more people. I want girls to see that they too can shred on guitar like the best of them and I want guys to see that they aren't the only ones. To do that, you need to take the business seriously and be creative with it, be open to finding a bigger audience and selling records, and find a way that works for your band to achieve these goals without compromising your integrity or ruining your friendship!

VC: What are some of your future goals as a guitarist and how do you plan on achieving them?

AR: Right now I'm practicing tapping. It's a new world for me and I plan on taking it slowly and learning the basics until I feel ready to move on up to the next phase, and the next after that. I like to constantly find challenges on the guitar that seem completely out of reach for me and then attack them full force until I master them to my satisfaction. There is no such thing as "I could never play that!" for anyone; it's all about doing it and having fun while you learn.

CONCLUSION

As you can see, there's a lot to learn if you want to be a professional guitarist. Just remember that learning music takes time. It is a journey, and you will never know everything there is to know. Even when you become a master, you will see unexplored territories over the horizon. But that is what makes it so exciting. Explore all the possibilities you can and continuously strive to grow as a musician.

Developing as a musician is two-fold. You are continually learning, and you are enjoying the journey along the way. So, always push for excellence, but check to make sure you are still having fun.

Good luck!